Rigby On Our Way to English

Writing Resource Guide

with *Writing Planner Masters*

Grade 1

TEXAS EDITION

Table of Contents

Introduction

Writers read their writing and revise it to shape their ideas and find their own voices as authors. Children, especially English language learners, need to be engaged in authentic writing experiences in order to learn how to write and to be writers who naturally and comfortably use the writing process. Because *On Our Way to English* focuses on informational writing, the Mini-lessons address primarily this form of writing.

This Writing Resource Guide consists of fifty-six Writing Mini-lessons written specifically for English language learners, as well as sixteen Writing Planners. These Mini-lessons and Writing Planners support you as a teacher of English language learners and are designed to let you model and teach the writing process as children are engaged in their roles as real writers.

The Mini-lessons should not be taught strictly in the sequence they appear. Rather, choose lessons from each of the five sections as you progress through the year. Pick and choose lessons as they are developmentally appropriate for children and for the "teachable moment." The comprehensive and detailed lesson plans ensure that you will be teaching the skills and strategies children need. The Mini-lessons include samples of modeling, think-alouds, skills, strategies, and options for activities especially tailored to the five Stages of Language Acquisition. You are encouraged to create your own modeling based on personal experiences and use the sample modeling as a springboard. In addition you can replace the sample modeled writing provided with writing of your own in order to personalize your lessons.

The Writing Resource Guide invites you to try new teaching strategies and techniques and explore many types of nonfiction writing, from labels and captions to simple sentences and paragraphs for the more advanced Stages. While these Mini-lessons focus on nonfiction writing, you are encouraged to supplement your lessons with a wide variety of literature from several sources, as within any enriching balanced literacy classroom.

We hope that you and the children in your classroom will enjoy discovering the power of writing.

About the Mini-Lessons

By learning the procedures, techniques, and skills that writers use during the writing process, English language learners make decisions about their writing as "real authors." The Writing Resource Guide Mini-lessons are organized according to the steps of the writing process. As shown in the chart below, these closely mirror the tasks and behaviors readers use before, during, and after reading.

Readers	Writers
Setting the Scene • activate and build prior knowledge • select topics and genre • determine purpose • consider audience of text • stimulate vocabulary	**Think! Think! Think!** • activate and build prior knowledge • select topics and genre • determine purpose • consider audience • stimulate vocabulary
Reading the Text • practice skills/strategies to read words • use strategies to create meaning • monitor meaning • use sensory images • build a flow of meaning	**Let's Get Started** • practice skills/strategies to transcribe words • use strategies to create meaning • monitor meaning • express sensory images • create a flow of ideas
Returning to the Text • ask questions • revisit text to revise meaning • strive for accuracy • focus on features of text • reflect to personalize text	**Making It Better** • ask questions • revisit text to clearly convey meaning and monitor English usage • strive for accuracy • return to text to examine features • reflect to personalize text
Responding to the Text • go beyond text to extend learning • share their responses • value the literature • express their voices • feel success • want to read the literature	**I'm an Author** • create a text which extends their thinking • share their writing • value their own compositions • establish their voices • feel success • want to reread their writing

STAGES ①②③④⑤

The Mini-lessons are organized into five sections that follow the steps of the writing process. (See pages 8–9 for further explanation.) Each Mini-lesson suggests Stages for which the Mini-lesson is appropriate, as well as how the lesson can be modified to accommodate English language learners in different Stages within your classroom.

You Will Need

A materials list is provided for every Mini-lesson.

Teacher Tip

Teacher Tips serve as reminders to modify, build on, and revisit the Mini-lessons as often as necessary.

Each of the fifty-six Mini-lessons has a clearly defined focus and a supportive teaching sequence. The Mini-lessons can be presented in small groups or with the entire class.

Let's Get Started
STAGES ①②③④⑤

Mini-lesson 10
Drawing/Talking About the Pictures

You Will Need
- ✔ large teacher journal or easel pad
- ✔ markers
- ✔ children's journals
- ✔ pencils

Teacher Tip
Use this Mini-lesson to build on your shared writing lessons whenever the opportunity arises in the classroom.

Assessment Connection
As you observe children writing, notice which children tend to write with pictures and which children use letters and words. Encourage children to try new ways of writing. For example, if they are only drawing pictures, ask them to try to write the initial sounds of words.

Lesson Background

Drawing pictures is recognized as a legitimate form of written expression. It is not merely a transitional phase before beginning to write words. It is important for children to feel their pictures are valued, contain important details, and have meaning. This is especially important for those English language learners in Stages 1 and 2 because many times this is the only way they are able to communicate.

Teaching the Lesson

- *Sometimes when I want to write something, I draw the picture first and then write words that tell about it. First I have to think of something to draw.* Point to your head and close your eyes. *Sometimes when I close my eyes, I can think of a picture better.* Close your eyes and demonstrate this process. *I am thinking about a ball.*
- Open your eyes and start drawing a picture of a ball in your teacher journal or on the easel pad. *Wait, I wasn't just thinking about a plain ball . . . It was a soccer ball!* Make your plain ball look like a soccer ball. If possible, show the children a real soccer ball.
- *Now I need to write some words to tell about my picture.* Point to your eyes and the soccer ball. *I'll write, I see a soccer ball. Do my words tell about my picture? Does my picture tell about my words?* Point to each as you talk about them. *Yes, the words and the picture match.* Close the large teacher journal or take down easel pad.

Extending the Lesson

If time permits, choose one child to demonstrate the process with the entire class.

On Your Own

Think of a picture in your mind and draw it in your journal (or on a piece of paper). Tell children that it is acceptable to begin by drawing the picture first and then writing the words, or they can begin with the words and then draw the picture. *When you are the writer, you get to decide what you want to do.*

Options for STAGES

| ❶ Have children in this Stage simply draw the picture. | ❷❸❹❺ Have children in these Stages draw the picture and then write the words. Some children may have to dictate the words to you. |

Options for Stages

Children in your classroom are probably not all at the same Stage of Language Acquisition. Therefore, it is important to provide options for the English language learners in the Stages designated as appropriate for a Mini-lesson. (See pages 12 and 13 for a complete explanation of the Stages of Language Acquisition.)

Many of the Mini-lessons can be used with learners in all Stages of Language Acquisition, while others are specific to children within the more advanced stages.

Let's Get Started
STAGES ❶❷❸❹❺

Mini-lesson 10
Drawing/Talking About the Pictures

You Will Need
✔ large teacher journal or easel pad
✔ markers
✔ children's journals
✔ pencils

Teacher Tip
Use this Mini-lesson to build on your shared writing lessons whenever the opportunity arises in the classroom.

Assessment Connection
As you observe children writing, notice which children tend to write with pictures and which children use letters and words. Encourage children to try new ways of writing. For example, if they are only drawing pictures, ask them to try to write the initial sounds of words.

Lesson Background
Drawing pictures is recognized as a legitimate form of written expression. It is not merely a transitional phase before beginning to write words. It is important for children to feel their pictures are valued, contain important details, and have meaning. This is especially important for those English language learners in Stages 1 and 2 because many times this is the only way they are able to communicate.

Teaching the Lesson
- *Sometimes when I want to write something, I draw the picture first and then write words that tell about it. First I have to think of something to draw.* Point to your head and close your eyes. *Sometimes when I close my eyes, I can think of a picture better.* Close your eyes and demonstrate this process. *I am thinking about a ball.*
- Open your eyes and start drawing a picture of a ball in your teacher journal or on the easel pad. *Wait, I wasn't just thinking about a plain ball . . . It was a soccer ball!* Make your plain ball look like a soccer ball. If possible, show the children a real soccer ball.
- *Now I need to write some words to tell about my picture.* Point to your eyes and the soccer ball. *I'll write,* I see a soccer ball. *Do my words tell about my picture? Does my picture tell about my words?* Point to each as you talk about them. *Yes, the words and the picture match.* Close the large teacher journal or take down easel pad.

Extending the Lesson
If time permits, choose one child to demonstrate the process with the entire class.

On Your Own
Think of a picture in your mind and draw it in your journal (or on a piece of paper). Tell children that it is acceptable to begin by drawing the picture first and then writing the words, or they can begin with the words and then draw the picture. *When you are the writer, you get to decide what you want to do.*

Options for STAGES
| ❶ Have children in this Stage simply draw the picture. | ❷❸❹❺ Have children in these Stages draw the picture and then write the words. Some children may have to dictate the words to you. |

Lesson Background
Discusses the writing development and background of Grade 1 English language learners and explains the purpose of the lesson.

Teaching the Lesson
Explicitly explains procedures for teaching the lesson, including how to model, question, and encourage English language learners to share their thoughts and ideas.

Extending the Lesson
This section provides more suggestions on how to help children understand the lesson.

On Your Own
Children need to work independently on what they have learned in the Mini-lesson to further help with understanding.

Assessment Connection
This informal assessment will help you evaluate children's writing samples and behavior during the lessons. In addition to this assessment provided in every Mini-lesson, there are two formal assessment forms in this book: the Writing Rubric on pages 18–19 and the Letter Formation Record on page 95.

The Mini-lessons in the Writing Resource Guide show you how to model techniques that will help English language learners manage their writing logically.

Think! Think! Think! (Prewriting): pages 23–30

Writers have to think when they plan their writing. During prewriting writers generate ideas, decide on a topic, determine their writing purpose, and consider the audience for their writing. With the "Think! Think! Think!" prewriting Mini-lessons, children learn how to make these prewriting decisions as developmentally appropriate to their Stages. They plan for writing and practice ways to organize their ideas on paper. This is especially important for English language learners, who need to generate relevant vocabulary before attempting to write.

Let's Get Started (Drafting): pages 31–56

Writers develop their own unique ways of getting started on a writing project. They bring their interests, knowledge of chosen topics, experiences with written language, and reading experiences to the process. As they begin writing, they also learn what else they may need to find out about the topic, as well as the structures and conventions of written language.

During the "Let's Get Started" Mini-lessons, English language learners begin to learn that drafting is a way to get started, a time to focus on thoughts, ideas, and meaning—a safe place to learn about written language. To guide children as they begin to draft, these Mini-lessons introduce the logistics of writing.

By observing and conferencing with children as they are drafting, you will be able to identify relevant learning needs and select from Mini-lessons that teach appropriate capitalization, punctuation, spelling, and grammar skills. As children move further into their writing projects, these Mini-lessons help them organize and develop the flow of their ideas. The draft becomes a real working copy, not just a "step" in the writing process.

Making It Better (Revising): pages 57–73

Writers learn as they read, share, and evaluate their writing. They ask themselves questions as they review and revise their pieces. Writers take time to reflect on the content of the message they are working hard to communicate. They also read for clarity and accuracy, to ensure that others can understand their writing. Writers need time to share, ask questions, and process responses as they work with their peers and with you.

The Writing Resource Guide's "Making It Better" Mini-lessons for "Content" help children learn how to solicit input from others and to look critically at their own writing. Children share their works-in-progress with a peer or a group, listening to each other and asking questions. With the Mini-lessons, children focus on editing for content to make their writing richer and clearer, which will ultimately help them find their own voices as writers.

The "Making It Better" Mini-lessons for "Mechanics" direct children as they edit their work for specific capitalization and punctuation skills, sentence structure, and spelling. English language learners are encouraged to use self-evaluation of their English usage to improve their writing. As children read, reflect, and share, they realize the power revision has to improve their writing and empower them as individuals with valuable ideas worth sharing and preserving.

I'm an Author (Publishing): pages 74–78

The "I'm an Author" Mini-lessons invite young writers to become contributing members of the literacy community in your classroom and beyond. Children review their own pieces to decide if they want to publish and how they want to publish. After writers choose the pieces they want to publish, they polish their work and craft a finished product. Sharing a finished piece becomes a celebration for the author and for the class.

About the Shared Writing Cards

In a balanced literacy program, children learn how to write through shared writing experiences. Teachers use the Shared Writing Cards to model the writing process.

Each Shared Writing Card features a graphic organizer. The graphic organizer is a visual support used to organize concepts during prewriting. The graphic organizer featured on each Shared Writing Card has realistic illustrations with lines underneath. As the class discusses the concepts shown in the graphic organizer, they generate and dictate language that the teacher records on the lines beneath each illustration. In the next step of the shared writing process, the teacher guides the class in using the language recorded on the Shared Writing Card to create an entire piece of writing. Observing the modeled process from graphic organizer to finished piece empowers children in their own use of graphic organizers to support their writing.

On the back (Side B) of each Shared Writing Card, there is a blank graphic organizer. The format of the graphic organizer is identical to the format on Side A. After using the illustrated graphic organizer on the front of the card (Side A), the graphic organizer on the back can be used to support writing on a new topic determined by the class. The class brainstorms a topic and then creates illustrations in the spaces provided based on the selected topic.

There is a Shared Writing Card for each of the eight units in first grade. Each Shared Writing Card is related to the unit theme and uses a different graphic organizer. To emphasize the reading-writing connection, each Shared Writing Card is inspired by an element of the Big Book.

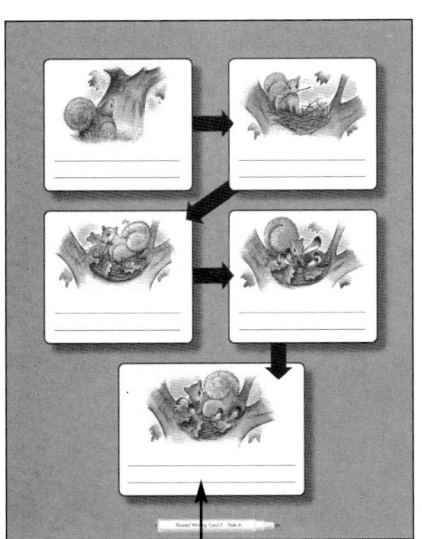

Side A
Lines beneath each illustration allow space to record phrases generated by children. Write-on, wipe-off format makes the Shared Writing Card reusable! Topic relates to the unit theme, "Animals and Their Homes."

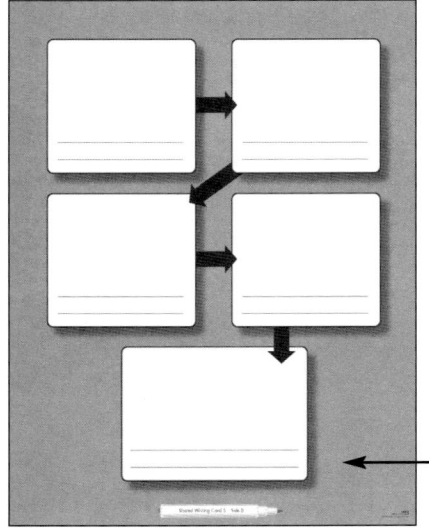

From Grade 1, Unit 5:
"Animals and Their Homes"

Side B
Children draw their own illustrations on a class-generated topic with the blank graphic organizer.

About the Writing Planners

The Writing Planners are reproducible graphic organizers that children use, first in groups and then individually, to develop concepts during prewriting. Before children use the Writing Planners, they have participated in the shared writing process with the teacher using the Shared Writing Card. Writing Planner A duplicates the graphic organizer used on the Shared Writing Card. Children use the Writing Planner in the same way they used the Shared Writing Card together during Shared Writing.

Children with limited language ability who are not able to write an entire piece can still use the Writing Planner. They can draw pictures and write words beneath, as they are able. When their language ability improves, they can move to the next step of writing an entire piece.

Each Shared Writing Card has a Writing Planner to go with it. Each Writing Planner has two versions, A and B. Writing Planner A is a reduced version of the back of the Shared Writing Card. Writing Planner B is a simplified version of Writing Planner A.

Writing Planner from Grade 1 Unit 5

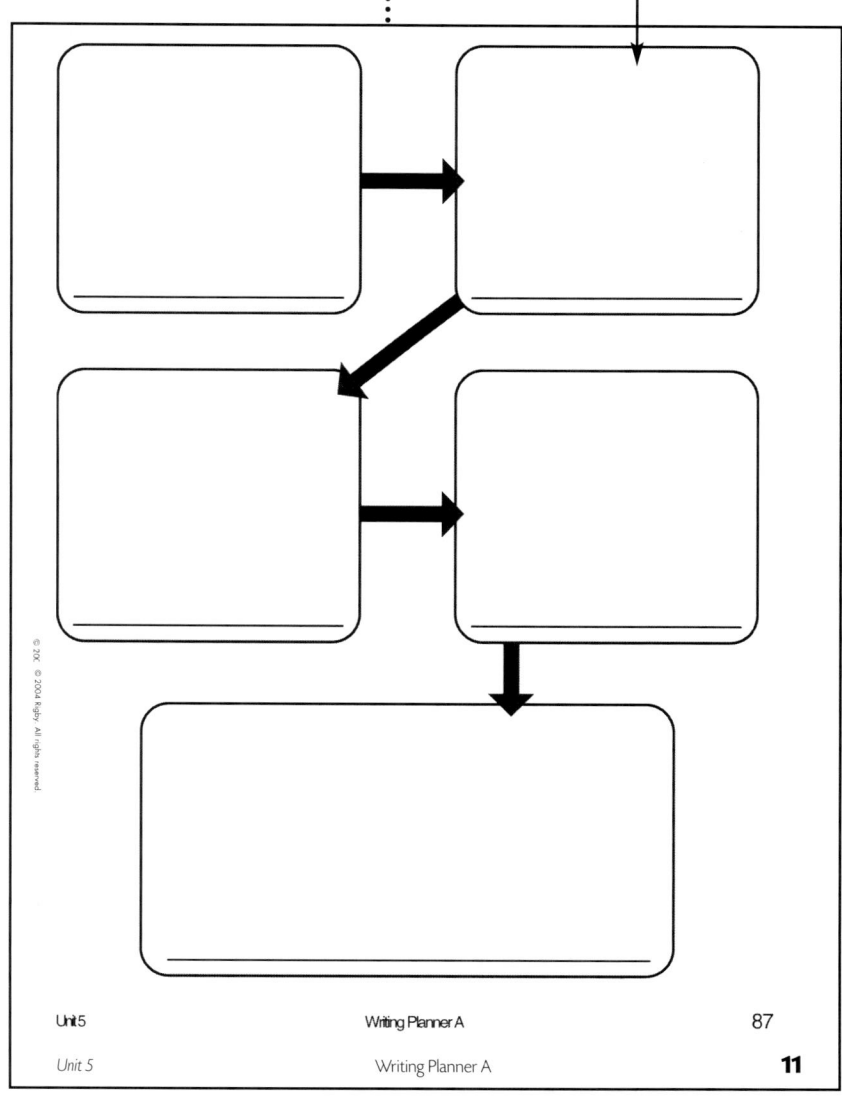

Unit 5   Writing Planner A   87

Unit 5   Writing Planner A   **11**

The Five Stages of English Language Acquisition ①②③④⑤

Teacher Tip

The Options for Stages section of the Mini-lesson will offer two to three suggestions for adapting the activity to different stages of English language acquisition. Refer to the chart here when determining each child's stage.

① Preproduction

Children in this stage...

- respond primarily nonverbally.
- display limited comprehension.
- manipulate objects or things to communicate.
- observe storytelling, shared reading, chanting, and singing.
- rely heavily on pictures in shared reading.
- participate in shared-to-guided reading.

During writing, children....

- should be able to communicate through pictures.
- may be able to write in their native languages.
- will be in the Emergent Level of literacy.

② Early Production

Children in this stage...

- use some basic words and simple phrases.
- express needs and preferences with routine language expressions.
- memorize rhymes, songs, and chants.
- manipulate objects to communicate.
- begin to comprehend storytelling, shared reading, chanting, and singing.
- rely heavily on pictures in shared reading.
- participate in shared-to-guided reading.
- participate in language-experience situations.

During writing, children....

- should be able to communicate through pictures.
- can probably write labels or a few words.
- may be able to dictate to you.
- may be in the Emergent or Early Level of literacy.

3 Speech Emergence

Children in this stage. . .
- participate in everyday conversations about familiar topics.
- produce longer, complete phrases and sentences with errors that hinder comprehension.
- display increasing comprehension.
- actively participate in shared reading/writing and guided reading.
- rely on high-frequency words and known sentence patterns in shared reading.
- participate in heavily scaffolded guided writing with strong teacher support.
- begin to approximate independent reading.

During writing, children. . . .
- may be able to write phrases or simple sentences.
- may have to dictate to you.
- may be at any Literacy Level in reading, but writing will resemble their spoken output.

4 Intermediate Fluency

Children in this stage. . .
- engage in ordinary conversations with more complex sentences and phrases.
- make errors that do not hinder comprehension.
- begin to use multiple strategies to construct meaning from print.
- actively participate in shared reading/writing, guided reading/writing, and independent reading.

During writing, children. . . .
- may be able to write complete sentences with errors according to their Literacy Levels.
- may be at any Literacy Level in reading and writing.

5 Advanced Fluency

Children in this stage. . .
- produce language comparable to that of a native speaker.
- actively use academic language to negotiate meaning.
- use multiple strategies to construct meaning from print.
- actively participate in all areas of balanced literacy, both reading and writing.

During writing, children. . .
- may be able to write complete sentences with few errors, according to their Literacy Levels.
- may be at any Literacy Level in reading and writing.

Writing in a Balanced Literacy Classroom

In a balanced literacy first-grade classroom with a supportive learning environment, children read, write, speak, listen, and observe through authentic literacy experiences:

- The diverse lives, personalities, and learning needs of each child are valued and respected.
- Children are immersed in many types of books and print.
- All children are viewed as learners and view themselves as learners.
- Children learn to read, write, and work together, as well as individually.
- There is time for practicing, sharing, and responding.
- Children's voices are heard as they make reading and writing choices, while taking steps toward becoming independent learners.

The Writing Resource Guide is designed to engage English language learners in real-life writing experiences within the context of a balanced literacy approach. Each of the balanced literacy approaches—modeled, shared, interactive guided, and independent—involves different degrees of learner responsibility and teacher support. In general, learning experiences are structured to occur in small and whole groups, with a gradual move toward independence.

English language learners are busy thinkers as they learn to write. They wonder about what to write about, puzzle about how to write to make their message clear, and think about how to organize their writing. They write, draw, and talk about their writing to make and maintain meaning. Within the supportive literacy experiences launched by the Writing Resource Guide, children learn to develop a sense of purpose for their writing, how to consider their audiences, and how to express their own voices.

Using Read-Alouds and Think-Alouds as Models for Writing

Using read-alouds and think-alouds models fluent reading behaviors for children and introduces beginning writers to various texts. Sharing aloud thoughts, feelings, and observations while you read and write helps English language learners understand the writing process as it occurs. In the Mini-lessons, think-aloud prompts are provided to help you focus on the purpose of the lesson.

Using Modeled Writing and Shared Writing

Modeled Writing

Modeled writing allows you to demonstrate the writing process by thinking aloud while composing a text on the board or on an easel pad. Focus on a brief piece of writing that relates to real-life experiences. Modeled writing is used within the Mini-lessons to show children how to make decisions about content, whether by drawing pictures or writing phrases or simple sentences. The short ten- to twenty-minute Mini-lessons presented in this book are the perfect way to keep modeled writing brief and focused on the skill or strategy you are teaching at a particular time.

Shared Writing

Shared writing is invaluable to English language learners in that it allows them to see the actual process of writing, allows them to share their own ideas in a supportive environment, and helps them see writing strategies in progress. In shared writing, the teacher serves as a scribe while children take the primary responsibility for the learning, creating, and writing. They work together supportively to compose and read the text. In *On Our Way to English*, the Shared Writing Cards also model the use of graphic organizers, a key step in the writing process for English language learners who need to generate vocabulary connected to a topic before attempting to write.

Tips for Reading Aloud

- Select books that interest children.

- Always practice reading the book and doing a think-aloud before reading to children.

- Keep the read-aloud book in the classroom to help children make reading and writing connections. The book can always be used as a convenient and familiar writing model.

Teacher Tip

A Mini-lesson should only last from ten to twenty minutes. Keep the modeled writing short and focused on the skill or strategy featured in the Mini-lesson.

Using Language Experience

Language experience writing is an authentic writing activity based on the melding of children's language and their life experiences. Language experience writing comes directly from children's own experiences as you, the teacher, scribe their words on paper. The writing piece becomes an interesting text for children because it is written by and for them. Although you are modeling the writing, the responsibility for developing the content and for reading the text is released to children. In the Writing Resource Guide, language experience writing is composed about common classroom experiences and used to model writing skills and strategies.

Using Interactive and Guided Writing

Interactive

From shared writing, an eventual and natural evolution toward interactive writing will occur, with children taking on a more active role in the writing process—children write on an easel pad or on the board as you provide supportive instruction within the "teachable moment."

Guided Writing

Interactive writing serves as a way to explicitly teach and practice specific writing and spelling skills. Guided writing allows English language learners to choose their own topics and support one another through a level of sharing and responding. Their writing pieces may also be extensions of guided, shared, or independent reading. As children are writing, you may consult with them about relevant writing process skills and strategies.

Using Independent Writing

Independent writing empowers writers and is the ultimate goal of all writing instruction. The writing ideas and extensions within the Mini-lessons and in the Writing Strategy Cards invite English language learners to explore writing in a way they may never have been able to do before. The step-by-step scaffolding process in *On Our Way to English* takes children from shared writing to peer-group writing to independent writing with familiar tools and practiced strategies.

Phases of Spelling Development

Precommunicative Spelling Phase

- shows developing knowledge of alphabet
- may or may not have left-to-right directionality
- may not be readable by others
- uppercase and lowercase letters used indiscriminately
- uses random strings of symbols, letters, or invented symbols

Semi-Phonetic Spelling Phase

- some letter-sound correspondence
- abbreviated words
- letter-names used to represent sounds
- letters to represent sounds
- word segmentation
- left-to-right directionality

Phonetic Spelling Phase

- match between all letters and all essential sounds
- left-to-right directionality
- invented spellings rather than random attempts at words
- word segmentation and spatial orientation

Transitional Spelling Phase

- vowels appear in every syllable
- correct letters in incorrect sequence
- alternative spellings for same sounds in different words
- learned words used frequently

Correct Spelling Phase

- entire word spelled correctly
- knowledge of word structures, prefixes, suffixes, contractions, and compound words
- mastery of uncommon spelling patterns
- uses large body of known words

Teacher Tip

This page defines the five phases of spelling development. The English language learners in your classroom will probably fall under different phases. The reason for assessing their spelling is to discover where each individual child falls on a continuum of development. This knowledge allows you to determine where he or she needs to move next in order to continue to grow as a writer.

Writing Rubric for English Language Writers

Use the following writing rubric in evaluating the writing of your English language learners. The rubric was designed specifically with English language learners in mind and focuses on providing criteria for evaluating informational writing, the focus of the *On Our Way to English* program.

Writing Level 1	**Message and Content** Unable to respond or draws a picture or dictates a message (in English or primary language).
	Conventions of English May know the direction that print goes and use some conventional symbols in a random fashion.
Writing Level 2	**Message and Content** Copies environmental print or labels drawings or writes a simple message.
	Conventions of English Begins to use spacing between words and sound-symbol relationships to produce temporary spelling.
	Word Choice and Academic Language May use isolated academic terms in labeling or dictation.
Writing Level 3	**Message and Content** With the support of a graphic organizer and a topic about which he or she can produce connected oral discourse, the child produces phrases or sentences that convey a message on one topic.
	Conventions of English Uses sound-symbol relationships to spell and groups words in phrases or sentences. Begins to use uppercase and lowercase conventionally. May make spelling errors that reflect his or her nonnative English pronunciation or native-language spelling patterns.
	Word Choice and Academic Language If academic language is included, it is often used inappropriately or imprecisely.
	Fluency and Sentence Structure Phrases or sentences can generally be understood by adults but may be repetitive and simple. Word order may reflect native-language word order.

There are four areas of evaluation within the levels: Message and Content, Conventions of English, Word Choice and Academic Language, and Fluency and Sentence Structure. The first two writing levels use only some of these areas since all are not appropriate.

Writing Level 4	**Message and Content** With the support of a graphic organizer, the child produces a piece of writing that has a beginning, middle, and end, as well as sentences on a single topic. **Conventions of English** Spells words in common word families and uses most punctuation conventionally. **Word Choice and Academic Language** Shows a range of vocabulary and varied word choice with some academic language used appropriately. **Fluency and Sentence Structure** Word order generally reflects English word order. Sentences may be simple but complete and perhaps loosely connected to one another or run-ons.
Writing Level 5	**Message and Content** With the support of a graphic organizer, the child writes several paragraphs with cohesive structure and connected sentences. **Conventions of Spelling** Uses spelling and punctuation accurately. Uses verb tenses and first/third person appropriately. May experiment with more complex verb forms. **Word Choice and Academic Language** Selects vocabulary, including academic language, appropriately and according to audience and purpose. **Fluency and Sentence Structure** Uses some compound sentences with conjunctions. Begins to use connecting words, although perhaps, inconsistently or inappropriately.
Writing Level 6	**Message and Content** Writes several pages with paragraphs in logical sequence and descriptions that are coherently developed. **Conventions of English** Has control of conventions appropriate to grade level. Uses complex verb forms skillfully. **Word Choice and Academic Language** Uses a wide range of vocabulary appropriate to audience, purpose, and style. Uses grade-level academic language effectively. **Fluency and Sentence Structure** Uses a range of sentence structures, including complex sentences. Uses connecting words effectively.

Snapshots of Young English Language Writers

Appropriate Mini-Lessons from the Writing Resource Guide to use with this child are:

- What Is Writing? on page 24.

- Drawing/Talking About the Pictures on page 32.

- Directionality on pages 37–39.

While the English language learners in your classroom are engaged in authentic writing experiences within the Writing Resource Guide, your task is to observe their use of writing strategies, skills, and behaviors. Writing samples from young writers are powerful indicators of children's knowledge of written language. An analysis of writing samples gives you a "snapshot" of the child as a writer. Knowing what to look for in a writing sample is key to its value for assessment. This is a skill that improves with practice and with increased knowledge about literacy development. The following are samples of writing from English language learners that represent each of the six levels of the Writing Rubric.

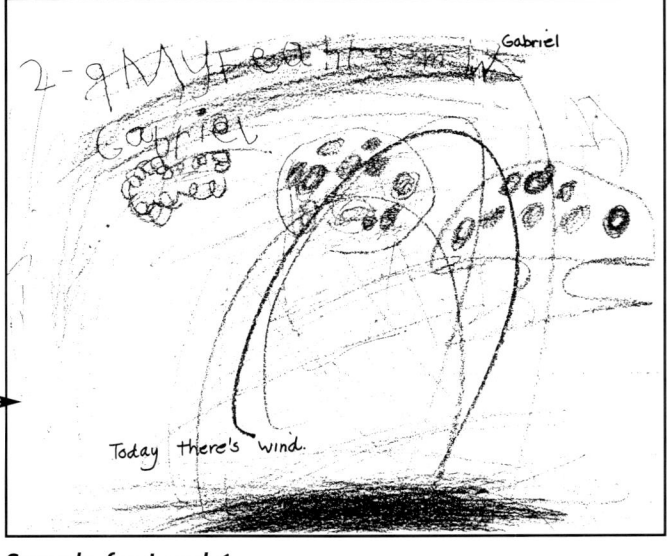

Sample for Level 1

Appropriate Mini-Lessons from the Writing Resource Guide to use with this child are:

- One-to-One Correspondence on page 42.

- Describing Words on page 55.

- Reading Your Work to Yourself on page 57.

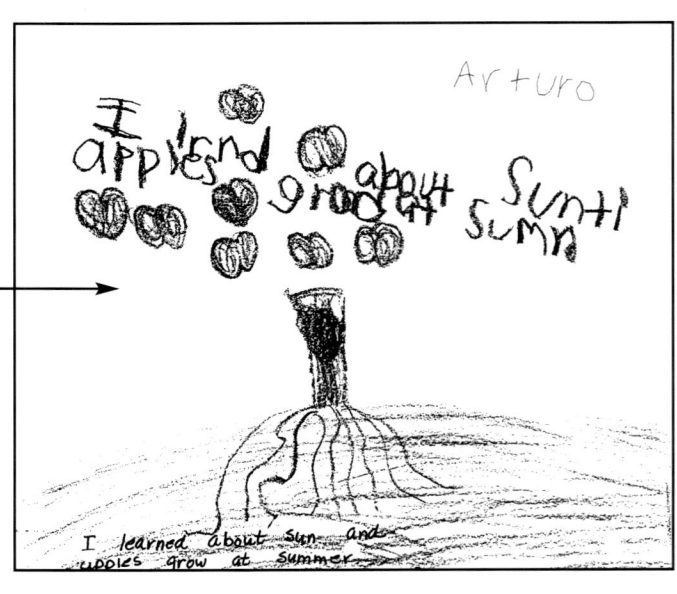

Sample for Level 2

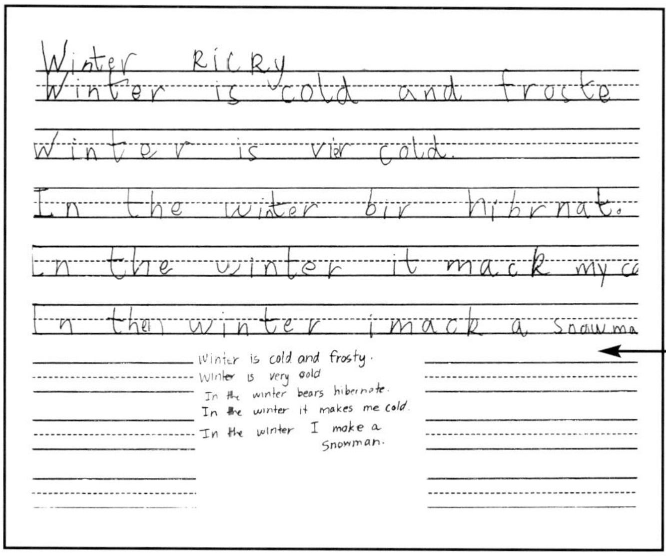

Sample for Level 3

Appropriate Mini-Lessons from the Writing Resource Guide to use with this child are:

- Copying Environmental Print on page 36.

- Using a Variety of Sentence Patterns on page 64.

- Using Writing Resources on page 70.

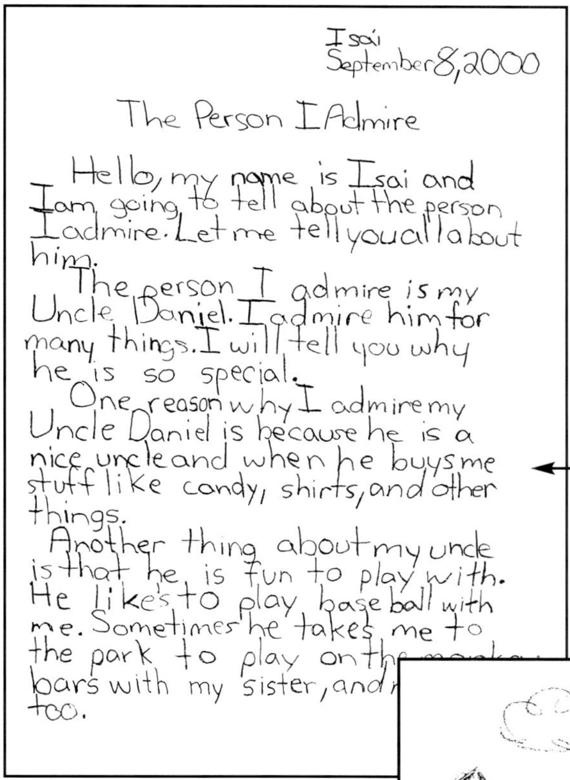

Samples for Level 4

Appropriate Mini-Lessons from the Writing Resource Guide to use with this child are:

- Copying Environmental Print on page 36.

- Describing Words on page 55.

- Reading Your Work to Yourself on page 57.

Appropriate Mini-Lessons from the Writing Resource Guide to use with this child are:

- Describing Words on page 55.

- Reading Your Work to Yourself on page 57.

- Asking for Comments on page 59.

Veronica
August 31/2000

My Community

My community is a special place. I will tell you about it. My neighbod has lots of streets with many houses. I have a school in front of my housey. My address is 55 West Bend. I have two neighbors. There names are Stela and Gloya there is a park, there houses away ob me. It has swings and and a slide. And in back of the school, there is a playgound. I told you about my community. I love it very much. And I hope to live there for a wile.

Samples for Level 5

Appropriate Mini-Lessons from the Writing Resource Guide to use with this child are:

- Adding Interesting Words on page 63.

- Using a Variety of Sentence Patterns on page 64.

- Choosing a Title on page 76.

01/16/2000

Pennsylvania is a Middle Colony that was founded in 1682. There are many reasons why people settled there. They had many good resources. They also made money many different ways.

There are many reasons why people settled in Pennsylvania. One of them is because Pennsylvania was offering religious toleration. They also went to Pennsylvania to escape from warm and to escape from slavery. They also went to Pennsylvania to make money and buy land.

Pennsylvania had many good resources. One of them is warm weather and they needed warm weather to keep horses and cows. They had good soil for farming and live stock. They also had lots of forests. They needed them for fur, lumber and wood. They had many rivers to transport to other places. They also transport by cutting trees and building boats.

They also made money many different ways. One of them is that they use to fish and sell it for money. They also made money by trooling. They would also make things and sell it to other people.

In conclusion there are many reasons why people settle in Pennsylvania. Pennsylvania also had many good

Samples for Level 6

Mini-lesson 1
What Is an Author?

Lesson Background

English language learners rarely think of themselves as authors. This Mini-lesson will teach children that anyone who writes anything is an author.

Teaching the Lesson

- Prior to the Mini-lesson, display the different written materials on a table. Hold up each one to show children. *Look at all of these things that I have.*
- Point to your eyes. *What do you see?* Have children tell you what each item is, if possible. *What is the same about all of these things?* Accept all responses. Help children understand that all of the items contain writing of some sort.
- Show children a pencil/marker/pen. *We write with these things. When someone writes something, he or she is an author.*
- Encourage children to say the word *author*. Point to the children. *You are all authors too.* Show the pen again. *Anyone who writes is an author.* Point to children. *Every time you write, you are an author.*

Extending the Lesson

Hold up two different papers, one with writing and one without. Have children point to the one an author wrote. Make sure all Stages of English language learners are participating.

On Your Own

Have children draw a picture of themselves in the act of writing. Show children a picture that you drew of yourself in the act of writing.

Options for STAGES

| ❶ Children in this Stage will simply draw pictures. | ❷ Children in this Stage can dictate a few words to you about what they are writing in the picture. After you write the words, tell children that they are now authors. | ❸❹❺ Tell children in these Stages that they can add words to their pictures too. *That will remind you that you are an author.* Some children may have to dictate a phrase or sentence to you. |

You Will Need

✔ assorted written materials: book, poem, list, letter, greeting card, postcard, advertising brochure, sheet music, and so on

Teacher Tip

Tailor the Mini-lesson to different Stages of English Language Acquisition and to the needs of the children in your classroom.

Assessment Connection

Note whether children understand that anyone who writes is an author.

TEKS **1.14F** understand literary terms (author, illustrator)
1.18A dictate messages
1.23B record or dictate own knowledge of a topic in various ways

Mini-lesson 2
What Is Writing?

You Will Need

✔ easel pad

✔ a picture of a cat (drawn by you) on an easel pad

✔ marker

✔ pencils

✔ writing paper; one per child

Lesson Background

It is the teacher's responsibility to focus children on print by modeling how print works and why writing is important. Children's print expressions may emerge as drawings, "lines and squiggles," random letters, labels, or sentences. Remember that English language learners may not have been exposed to "English print" before.

Teaching the Lesson

- Distribute pencils and writing paper. *What do you think we are going to do with these pencils and paper?* Elicit responses. *That's correct, we are going to write. How many of you know how to write? When I was young, like you, I liked to draw pictures.*

- Display an easel pad. *Here is a cat that looks like one I drew when I was little. I also liked to write about my pictures. At first I did this.* Make a few squiggly lines on the easel pad. *I could read my writing. I knew it said cat. Then I started making letters to go with my writing.* On the easel pad, write a *c. Cat starts with the letter* c. *Then I started writing whole words.* Write the word *cat* on the pad. *This is the word* cat. *When you start writing more, you will be able to put words in a sentence.* Write *My cat is big* on the easel pad. Point to each word as you read. *If you don't know the sounds of the letters, you can write squiggles, letters, or words.*

Teacher Tip

Revisit this Mini-lesson often until children show evidence of incorporating the instruction in their writing.

Extending the Lesson

Have children tell you a word or a sentence and demonstrate how to write it in different ways, as above.

On Your Own

Hold up a piece of paper and point to the top. *At the top of your paper, draw a picture of something you like to eat.* Move your mouth as if you are eating.

Assessment Connection

Date and save these writing samples. Later, have children look at their earlier work to see how they have progressed as writers.

Options for **STAGES**

❶Children in this Stage may only be able to draw pictures.	❷❸❹❺Children in these Stages can attempt to write about their pictures. They can use squiggles, letters, words, or sentences.

TEKS **1.17E** gain increasing control of penmanship
1.23B record or dictate own knowledge of a topic in various ways

Mini-lesson 3
Where Do We See Writing?

Lesson Background

We often take the amount of writing that surrounds us for granted. Part of encouraging English language learners to want to write begins with developing awareness of the amount of writing that surrounds us in our everyday lives. Children should understand that writing provides us with a multitude of useful and enjoyable functions. This Mini-lesson will help show children how important writing is in the real world.

Teaching the Lesson

Show children the examples of writing. Tell them that all of these are considered writing. Show children what English writing looks like. Ask them to look around the room for examples of English writing. Have children point to the different places they see written words.

Extending the Lesson

Options for **STAGES**

❶❷ Put children in pairs (mixing Stage 1 children with Stage 2) and have them find examples of English words in writing, such as the name of someone, the days of the week, and so on.

❸❹❺ Ask children in these Stages questions such as: *Why is it important that we know how to read the word* stop *on a stop sign?* or *Why should we notice the word* girls *on a bathroom door?* and so on.

On Your Own

Have children make name tags for themselves. Demonstrate how to make a name tag by writing *your* name. After you write your name, point to your name on the name tag, say your name, and point to yourself. Distribute pieces of card stock and ask children to write (or copy) their names. You may have to show children where they can find their names to copy them. Then they may decorate the name tags. Display the finished name tags on a wall, a bulletin board, or in a pocket chart. You can even take pictures of the children and place them next to their name tags. Encourage children to read and match names to faces.

You Will Need

✔ 2" x 3" card stock; one piece per child

✔ markers

✔ examples of writing from different languages, if possible

Assessment Connection

Notice when, and how often, children use, or attempt to use, environmental print.

TEKS **1.5A** recognize that print represents spoken language and conveys meaning
1.17A write own name and other important words
1.27H use print from the environment

Mini-lesson 4
Why Do People Write?

Lesson Background

Help English language learners see that there are many reasons to write. This Mini-lesson will make them aware of how people use writing to help them communicate.

Teaching the Lesson

- Point to a bag containing a piece of paper and a marker. Hold up two fingers. *I have two things in this bag that I can use to tell you what I'm thinking about.* Take the piece of paper from the bag. *How can this piece of paper tell you what I'm thinking about? What else would I need?*
- Take the marker from the bag. *Does anyone know how I can use the paper and the marker to help me tell you what I'm thinking about?* Accept all responses. *Yes, I can use the marker to write on the paper.*
- On the lined paper, write a simple sentence, such as *I am happy.* Point to the writing. *It says* I am happy.

Extending the Lesson

Options for STAGES

① ② Show children in these Stages the different types of writing. Explain that these are examples of things that people write, and that people write for different reasons. Hold up the grocery list and the letter and ask, for example, *Which one of these is a list?* or *Which one of these is a letter to someone?*

③ ④ ⑤ Say, *I wrote the sentence* I am happy, *to tell you how I feel. Can you think of other reasons to write?* Guide children to offer ideas, such as making lists to remember things, telling stories, saying thank-you for a gift, and so on. For each response offered, ask who might do the writing and why.

On Your Own

Have children draw a picture of someone they know in the act of writing. Show a picture that you have drawn of yourself writing. Encourage children to share their writing with someone at home.

Options for STAGES

① Have children in this Stage simply draw pictures.

② After drawing the pictures, have children in this Stage dictate a few words to you.

③ ④ ⑤ After drawing the pictures, have children in these Stages add phrases or sentences that tell why or what the people are writing. Some will be able to write sentences on their own. Others can dictate to you.

 **TEKS**
1.18C write to record ideas and reflections
1.18E write to communicate with a variety of audiences
1.18F write in different forms for different purposes
1.23B record or dictate own knowledge of a topic in various ways

Mini-lesson 5
Where Do I Write?

Lesson Background

Writers not only write for many reasons, they also write—and keep their writing—in many places. Journals, writing notebooks, and writing folders are all important tools for English language learners to understand and use.

Teaching the Lesson

- Prior to the lesson, make simple journals for children. For each, staple 10–12 sheets (full or half) of writing paper between construction paper covers.
- Display the commercially bound journal. *I want to show you something special today. This is my journal. It is a book. I write all of the things that I think about in this book.* Show children sample entries and read them a short excerpt, including the date. Make sure the entry is very simple to understand. Point to the date. *I always put the date at the top of my journal page.* Point to the top. *Later, when I go back and read it again, the date helps me remember when I wrote the words.*
- Flip through the rest of the journal and show all of the blank pages. *I will keep writing until I have written on every page. Then I will start a new journal.*

Extending the Lesson

Bring in examples of published journals to show children.

On Your Own

Show children the first page of a blank journal. Point to the top. *We are going to put the date at the top of the page. This is how we write the date.* Show children the format in which you want the date recorded. *I will give you an idea for writing in your journal, but you also can write about whatever you would like. Here is an idea.* On an easel pad, write a simple sentence starter, such as *Today I feel _____.* Elicit different feeling words from children, such as happy, sad, angry, and so on. Make sure your face demonstrates each feeling as it is said. *I want you to draw how you feel on your paper. When you are finished, you may color the front of your journal.*

Options for STAGES

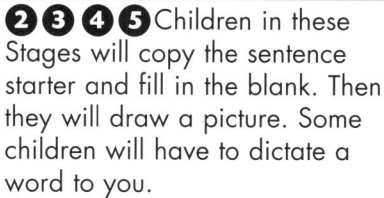

| ❶ Children in this Stage will simply draw pictures. | ❷❸❹❺ Children in these Stages will copy the sentence starter and fill in the blank. Then they will draw a picture. Some children will have to dictate a word to you. |

You Will Need

- ✔ commercially bound journal, preferably with some entries written by you
- ✔ writing paper journals; one per child
- ✔ crayons/markers
- ✔ pencils; one per child

Assessment Connection

Writing journals, notebooks, and folders offer a continuous assessment tool. You can use them to show parents how children's writing skills have progressed over time.

TEKS 1.18C write to record ideas and reflections

Mini-lesson 6

Getting Ideas

You Will Need

- ✔ easel pad
- ✔ markers
- ✔ writing paper; one per child
- ✔ an example of a list

Lesson Background

Just as adults do, children draw upon personal experiences for writing ideas. Encourage English language learners to think about what they know and do when they are looking for things to write about.

Teaching the Lesson

- *Do you ever think about where authors get their ideas?* Point to your head. *Sometimes authors use their imaginations, like when an author writes about cats that talk. Sometimes authors write about something that they can do, like draw.* Draw a picture of a house and then write *This is a house* under the picture. *There are a lot of different ideas, and that is why there are all kinds of writing. We are all authors, and we need to decide what to write about.*

- Hold up a pen/pencil/marker. *We'll make a list of ideas.* Show an example of a list. *First let's think of things that we know how to do.* On an easel pad write *I can _____. The beginning of this sentence says* I can . . . Now show children something that you can do, such as jump. Then fill in the blank. *I can <u>jump</u>. This sentence says* I can jump.

Teacher Tip

Keep anecdotal records about interests and experiences children reveal in classroom discussion. Use this information when choosing future writing topics.

Extending the Lesson

Let's write down some things you can do. Have the class come up with a list together. Choose 8–10 activities children can do and write them on an easel pad.

Options for STAGES

❶❷ Children in these Stages can demonstrate something that they can do.

❸❹❺ Children in these Stages can dictate to you something that they can do.

Look at all of your wonderful ideas! Any of your ideas would make a great piece of writing. Now you are going to write what you can do.

On Your Own

Write the words *I can* on the easel pad. *It says* I can . . . *Now draw a picture of something that you can do.*

Options for STAGES

❶ Have children in this Stage draw a picture. If you can, interpret the picture and write a phrase describing what they are doing.

❷❸❹❺ Have children in these Stages also copy the beginning of the sentence *I can* and write what they can do. Some children will be able to write on their own. Others may need to dictate to you.

Assessment Connection

Note whether children are able to easily think of ideas about what to write.

TEKS 1.18C write to record ideas and reflections
1.18F write in different forms for different purposes
1.19B generate ideas before writing on assigned tasks

Mini-lesson 7
Making an Idea List

Lesson Background

Children often engage in dramatic play at home and at school. When they do so, they may include writing lists as a part of that play. For instance, when they are in the kitchen area they may write a grocery list. In the office area, they may write a list of phone numbers. This Mini-lesson will validate English language learners' use of lists and show them how to use lists in their writing.

Teaching the Lesson

Show children the different lists. Discuss how these lists help people in their daily lives. Ask them to think about how their families use lists and have some volunteers share.

Extending the Lesson

With the class, brainstorm a list of writing ideas to which children can relate such as *going to the park* or *pets*. If possible, have Stage 1 children point to different items in the room that they could write about. Draw a simple picture symbol next to items on the list from the classroom to encourage emergent readers and writers to use this list later. Display the list in the room where children can see it.

On Your Own

Encourage children to use the class list when they are writing. A good time for this might be during journal writing. Children should also be encouraged to make their own idea lists. Have them keep their lists in a safe spot, such as their writing folders. Periodically remind children to add new ideas to their lists.

Options for **STAGES**

❶ Children in this Stage can create pictorial idea lists.

❷ ❸ ❹ ❺ Children in these Stages can create pictorial lists and add words to it if they are able.

You Will Need

✔ easel pad

✔ marker

✔ different types of lists: grocery, to-do, phone numbers, and so on

Assessment Connection

When talking with children about their writing, note those children who cannot think of ideas for writing on their own. Also note those children who readily share their idea lists with you. For Stage 1 children, picture symbols can count as ideas. Encourage children to talk with each other and share ideas.

TEKS **1.18F** write in different forms for different purposes
1.19A generate ideas before writing on self-selected topics

Mini-lesson 8
Tools Writers Use

You Will Need

✔ small self-stick notes; one or two per child

✔ bell

✔ easel pad

✔ marker

Teacher Tip

Expect children to identify any of the following:

✔ pens, pencils, markers, crayons

✔ paper

✔ computer

✔ typewriter

✔ picture dictionary

✔ tape (for binding)

✔ sentence strips

✔ pocket chart

✔ self-stick notes

✔ index cards

✔ books

Assessment Connection

While children are drawing and writing, note whether they are using the correct tools.

Lesson Background

There are many tools that writers use when they write. Some writers write in longhand, while others use a computer to do their writing. This lesson will key in English language learners to the kinds of tools they can use when they write.

Teaching the Lesson

Ask children if they know what a doctor is and if they have ever been to a doctor's office. Then ask them what kinds of things a doctor uses. Elicit responses and then, if possible, show children a stethoscope, tongue depressor, thermometer, and so on. Explain to children that these things a doctor uses are called *tools* or *instruments*. Lead the discussion to the idea that just as a doctor uses special tools, someone who writes does too.

Extending the Lesson

Tell children that they are going to look for tools that a writer might use in the classroom. Give each child one or two self-stick notes. Put your finger to your mouth to illustrate that they are to be quiet. Have them walk around the room finding tools and marking each tool with a sticky note. Demonstrate this process by putting a sticky note on a piece of chalk. Tell children to find as many different tools as possible. After about two minutes, ring a bell or say *Time's up.*

On Your Own

Have children gather in a circle. Let them share items they identified and list each on an easel pad, with a picture symbol next to it. (Do not list duplicates.)

Options for **STAGES**

❶ Children in this Stage can show you the different items.

❷❸❹❺ Children in these Stages can show and then tell you about the different items.

Discuss the items and how writers use each. If not all of the tools that you wanted children to find are mentioned, you can add to the list yourself. Explain why they are tools.

TEKS **1.19E** use technology to compose text

Putting Your Name and Date on Your Paper

Lesson Background

English language learners need to develop the habit of putting their names and the date on their writing. Doing so helps them take ownership of their work. It is also essential for assessing progress and for record keeping. Remember that the location of the name and date and the order in which the name is written (last name, first name) may be different in some languages.

Teaching the Lesson

- Hold up the two unlabeled items. *I just don't know who these things belong to. Why do you think that is? You are right. There are no names on these things. Each one could be Juan's or Peng's. I just don't know.*

- Hold up the two labeled items. *I can tell who these things belong to because one has Ana's name and one has Iman's name written on it. It is just as important to put your name on your writing as it is to put it on your notebooks and lunch box. Putting your name on your writing lets everyone know that you are the author. There is something else you need to put on all of your writing. You need to put the date on it. Later on you will be able to look back at your writing when you first started and see how much better you have become.*

Extending the Lesson

Have children practice writing their names and the date on the chalkboard.

Options for **STAGES**

❶ Have children in this Stage copy their names and the date.	❷❸❹❺ Have children in these Stages write their names and copy the date.

On Your Own

I am going to give each of you a sheet of writing paper. I will show you where to write your name. I will also show you where to put the date and how to write it. Then you can keep this paper in your writing folder to help you remember to put your name and the date on everything you write.

You Will Need

- ✔ two similar items, both without names (lunch boxes, notebooks, backpacks, and so on)
- ✔ two similar items, each labeled with owner's name
- ✔ writing paper; one sheet per child

Assessment Connection

Note children who have difficulty remembering to put their names and the date on papers. You may want to tape a visual reminder to their desks or have them add their names to several blank pages and store these in their folders to use at writing time.

TEKS **1.17A** write own name and other important words

Mini-lesson 10
Drawing/Talking About the Pictures

Lesson Background

Drawing pictures is recognized as a legitimate form of written expression. It is not merely a transitional phase before beginning to write words. It is important for children to feel their pictures are valued, contain important details, and have meaning. This is especially important for those English language learners in Stages 1 and 2 because many times this is the only way they are able to communicate.

Teaching the Lesson

- *Sometimes when I want to write something, I draw the picture first and then write words that tell about it. First I have to think of something to draw.* Point to your head and close your eyes. *Sometimes when I close my eyes, I can think of a picture better.* Close your eyes and demonstrate this process. *I am thinking about a ball.*
- Open your eyes and start drawing a picture of a ball in your teacher journal or on the easel pad. *Wait, I wasn't just thinking about a plain ball . . . It was a soccer ball!* Make your plain ball look like a soccer ball. If possible, show the children a real soccer ball.
- *Now I need to write some words to tell about my picture.* Point to your eyes and the soccer ball. *I'll write,* I see a soccer ball. *Do my words tell about my picture? Does my picture tell about my words?* Point to each as you talk about them. *Yes, the words and the picture match.* Close the large teacher journal or take down easel pad.

Extending the Lesson

If time permits, choose one child to demonstrate the process with the entire class.

On Your Own

Think of a picture in your mind and draw it in your journal (or on a piece of paper). Tell children that it is acceptable to begin by drawing the picture first and then writing the words, or they can begin with the words and then draw the picture. *When you are the writer, you get to decide what you want to do.*

Options for **STAGES**

❶ Have children in this Stage simply draw the picture.	❷❸❹❺ Have children in these Stages draw the picture and then write the words. Some children may have to dictate the words to you.

TEKS
1.18B write labels, notes, and captions
1.18C write to record ideas and reflections
1.19A generate ideas before writing on self-selected topics
1.23B record or dictate own knowledge of a topic in various ways

Directionality: Left-to-Right

Lesson Background
When English language learners begin writing, they are often unfamiliar with directionality. Many children from other cultures have languages that go from right to left, or vertically. Take this into consideration when teaching this lesson. It needs to be explained that in English we write from left to right.

Teaching the Lesson
- Show the different newspapers if possible. Explain that different cultures write differently.
- Explain that in English we begin writing on the left. *Everyone, hold up your left hand and make an L shape with your first finger and thumb.* Model this for children, making sure that you are not facing them as it may confuse them. *You can remember which hand is your left by looking at the L because* left *starts with the letter* L. *Today I am going to write about my family* (or any other topic). *I put a green dot at the beginning of each line to show where I begin.*
- Begin writing at the first green dot. *Green means go! That tells me where I should begin writing.* Continue saying "Green means go!" as you write.
- Read your writing to children when finished. *Did you see where I went when I got to the end of a line? I always started my writing at the left side of the page, next to the green dot.*

Extending the Lesson
Reread your writing to children and ask them to watch your finger point as you read. *Did you notice that when I finished reading a line, I went to the next green dot? I always begin at the left side of the paper when I read and write in English.*

On Your Own
Today as you write in your journals, I want you to do the same thing and begin on the left side. Remember the L that you made with your hand if you forget where to begin. For those students who need it, place green dots along the left sides of their papers.

Options for STAGES
| ❷❸ Children in these Stages may only be able to write a few words or a phrase. Some children may need to dictate to you. | ❹❺ Children in these Stages should try to write a sentence or two. Some children may need to dictate to you. |

You Will Need
- ✔ green marker or green dot stickers
- ✔ black marker
- ✔ writing paper
- ✔ pointer
- ✔ familiar Big Book
- ✔ if possible, newspapers in different languages where print and directionality are different from English, such as Chinese, Japanese, Hebrew, and so on

Assessment Connection
Note which children are still having difficulty with directionality. You may want to mark and reproduce writing paper with visual cues that show where to begin and continue writing.

TEKS **1.5B** know that print moves left-to-right and top-to-bottom
1.17D write messages that move left-to-right and top-to-bottom
1.27B recognize directionality of English reading

Mini-lesson 16
Directionality: Top-to-Bottom

You Will Need

- ✔ familiar Big Book with multiline text
- ✔ pointer
- ✔ easel pad
- ✔ marker
- ✔ writing paper; one per child
- ✔ children's writing journals
- ✔ writing folder; one per child

Teacher Tip

Revisit this Mini-lesson often until children show evidence of incorporating the instruction in their writing.

Assessment Connection

Note which children continue to have difficulty with top-to-bottom writing. See how this corresponds to their knowledge of print conventions when reading. You may want to make and reproduce writing paper that has visual cues to remind writers about correct directionality.

Lesson Background

When English language learners begin writing, they may have problems with directionality. Children at this age often write from bottom-to-top and right-to-left because they do not understand how to use space for writing. This Mini-lesson helps model correct directionality. Refer to Mini-lesson 15, "Left-to-Right," on page 37 for additional instruction on directionality.

Teaching the Lesson

Reread a familiar Big Book to children using a pointer. Ask them to watch where your pointer starts as you begin to read. After reading one page, discuss the concept of top-to-bottom reading. Continue reading several more pages with the pointer. Ask volunteers to show you where to begin reading each time you start a new page.

Extending the Lesson

Distribute writing paper to children. Ask them to write their names and the date, as they have learned to do in their journals. Then have them place a green dot on the paper to show where they would begin writing. Demonstrate the following on paper for children to copy. Have them draw arrows to show the way their words would travel across and down the page. You may want children to keep this paper as a visual reminder in their writing folders.

On Your Own

Have children write in their journals. Remind children that writers begin writing at the top of the writing space and work down to the bottom. Note: You may want to point out that when including drawings in their pieces, they should begin writing in the middle of the page and leave space at the top.

Options for **STAGES**

② ③ Children in these Stages may write a few words or a phrase and include a picture. Children may need to dictate their words or phrases to you.

④ ⑤ Children in these Stages should try to write a sentence or two. Children may need to dictate their sentences to you.

TEKS 1.5B know that print moves left-to-right and top-to-bottom
1.17D write messages that move left-to-right and top-to-bottom
1.27B recognize directionality of English reading

38 *On Our Way to English*

Directionality: Return Sweep

Lesson Background

When English language learners are beginning to write, their writing often appears all over the page. Just as children learn that we read from left to right, they must learn that when they write they start at the left, write to the end of the line, and then move down to the beginning of the next line. Remember that in other languages the directionality may be different.

Teaching the Lesson

- Remind children that when we write in English, we always begin at the left side of the page and write our words in a line going across the page to the right side. When we get to the end of the line at the right side of the page, we move our pencils down a line and begin at the left side again.

- Tell children that together you are going to write the Daily News. Ask for someone to tell you about something that happened to him or her the night before. Sum up what the child is saying in a short sentence, such as "Maria went to the grocery store with her mom last night." Then put your marker on the left side of the paper. *I'm going to write what Maria said. I'm putting my marker on the left side of the paper.* Slowly write the sentence, making sure that you run to the end of the line before you finish the sentence. As you get near the right edge of the paper, ask children to predict whether you will have enough room to write the next word.

- *Since I'm at the end of this line, I will move my marker down a line and write the rest of the sentence here.* Then begin writing the remainder of the sentence under the first line, beginning at the same point on the left side of the paper.

Extending the Lesson

If you have time, ask for volunteers to add to your Daily News.

Options for **STAGES**

❷❸ Children in these Stages might tell you a few words or a phrase. As you write, turn their words into a sentence.	❹❺ Children in these Stages should describe events in complete sentences.

On Your Own

Have children open their writing journals. Model the following on your own paper. *Today, before you begin writing in your journals, use a green crayon to make a dot to remind yourself where to begin. Make another dot on the second line to show where you will go when you reach the end of the first line. Try to write something that takes up at least two lines on your journal page.* Some children may have to dictate to you. If this is the case, have them tell you where to write.

You Will Need

- ✔ easel pad
- ✔ marker
- ✔ children's writing journals
- ✔ green crayon; one per child

Assessment Connection

Observe children as they write to see if they are beginning to use correct directionality automatically. Repeat this Mini-lesson and the other directionality Mini-lessons on pages 37 and 38 with children who need additional help.

TEKS **1.17B** write each letter of the alphabet, using correct formation, size, and spacing
1.17F use word and letter spacing and margins
1.18A dictate messages

Mini-lesson 18
Letters and Words

Lesson Background

When English language learners first begin to write, they often do not understand the difference between letters and words. They may write a letter *m* and tell you that it is the word *me*. Children need to understand that there are 26 letters in the alphabet, and when letters are grouped together in specific ways, they make words. Many other languages have pictures as words or have a completely different lettering system. Please be aware of this as you are teaching this lesson.

Teaching the Lesson

• Hand out the alphabet cards in order, one per child. Have each child, as he or she gets a card, stand in line at the front of the room. If there are not 26 children, keep the extra cards. If there are more than 26 children, they can take turns with the more commonly used letters. Give children in Stages 1 and 2 letters that fall in the middle of the alphabet so that they can see how children in the more advanced stages demonstrate this activity.

• Point to each child as you call out his or her letter. Reinforce the concept that a letter is different from a word.

• Now choose one of the children's names to use as an example: *Carlos*. Write the name *Carlos* on an easel pad or on the board. Ask that the six children who are holding the cards for the letters C-A-R-L-O-S step away from the line. Spread apart the children who have the letters of Carlos's name. Tell the rest of the children that these are letters when they are separated. Then have those same children stand close together in the correct order. Tell children that these six letters together make a word, *Carlos*.

Extending the Lesson

Use a few other names and continue the process. If there is time and children are enthusiastic, try proceeding with the activity using a few words from your Word Wall.

On Your Own

Encourage children to write in their journals about an activity they enjoy.

Options for STAGES

❶ Children in this Stage can draw a picture and write their name beneath it. Have them count the number of letters in their name.	❷❸ Children in these Stages can label their picture with a few words or a phrase. Have them count the number of words they use.	❹❺ Children in these Stages can write a sentence about their picture. Have them count the number of words they use.

Invented/Developmental Spelling

Lesson Background

Some English language learners write without hesitation, using scribbles, letters, and sometimes words to write. Others have no idea how to go about this mysterious process of writing. This Mini-lesson models the act of writing for children.

Teaching the Lesson

- Put on your "first-grade hat." *Today I have on my "first-grade hat." As I write for you, I am going to write like I might have written when I was your age.*
- Point to yourself. *I know that when I was in first grade, I had to think hard about how to spell the words when I wrote.*
- Begin to write on an easel pad. *As I write, I know I have to say my words out loud and stretch them out like a rubber band.* You may want to demonstrate using a real rubber band. *When I say my words slowly, I can hear the sounds better. I want to write* I like my school. Point to yourself. *I know how to write the word* I, *so that's easy. Now I'll think about* like. As you write the word *like*, say the sounds as you write them. Do not include the letter *e* at this time, because it is silent. When you get to the word *school*, you may write it as *skul* or *skool*. If you choose the latter, you may connect the *-oo* to *boo*, *zoo*, or *moo* for the children. (The modeling of invented/developmental spelling may be something to share with parents.)
- Model the following. *After I write, I need to go back and read what I wrote. The words on the paper help me figure out what I should write next.*

Extending the Lesson

If there is time, add more sentences. You can have children help you with the sounds.

On Your Own

Today when you write, say your words out loud and stretch them out to hear the sounds. Write all the letter sounds you hear. Then read your writing to yourself.

Options for **STAGES**

❷❸ Children in these Stages may only write a few words or phrases.	❹❺ Children in these Stages should be encouraged to write a complete sentence.

Some children may still need to dictate sentences to you. If this is the case, have them try to help you with the sounds.

Assessment Connection

See page 17 for a discussion on the phases of spelling development. You may want to use the developmental spelling phases to analyze a child's writing. When planning for an individual conference with that child, make a note of one teaching point related to the child's developmental spelling, or note patterns you see among children in your class and develop further Mini-lessons.

TEKS **1.5H** understand that spoken words are represented by specific sequences of letters
1.6F segment one-syllable spoken words into individual phonemes
1.17C use phonological knowledge to write messages

Mini-lesson 20
One-to-One Correspondence

You Will Need

- ✔ craft sticks/tongue depressors
- ✔ markers/crayons
- ✔ individual books for children
- ✔ easel pad
- ✔ teacher pointer
- ✔ two simple sentences written on an easel pad

Lesson Background

As English language learners become competent readers and writers, they must develop their understanding of spacing between words. This will help them better understand one-to-one correspondence. These two concepts should be modeled frequently for children.

Teaching the Lesson

- Hold up the pointer. *I have written two sentences. Watch the pointer as I read.* Leave the pointer at the beginning of the line as you read the first sentence. As you read the second sentence, follow along with the pointer, reading and pointing to each word. *Did you notice that the first sentence was harder for me to figure out because I wasn't pointing to each word?*
- Point to the second sentence. *When I read the second sentence, I pointed to each word. That made it a lot easier to read this sentence. Every time you read a word in a sentence, you should be able to point to a word either with your finger* (hold up a finger) *or a pointer* (hold up a craft stick/pencil/tongue depressor). *As you are reading words you have written and pointing to them, be sure that you have one word written for every word you read. Also make sure that when you write, every word you want to say is written down.*

Teacher Tip

Use this Mini-lesson to build on your shared writing lessons whenever the opportunity arises in the classroom.

Extending the Lesson

- Have children decorate their own pointers. You can use craft sticks or tongue depressors. Make sure you write children's names on them in case they get lost.
- Have children come up and use their pointers to point to the words as you read a book or poem.

On Your Own

Assessment Connection

As children are reading their work back to you, be sure that they have a word written for every word they read.

Options for STAGES

❷❸ Have children in these Stages write a few words or phrases and have them read them back to you, pointing to each word as they read.	❹❺ Have children in these Stages try to write a sentence or two and have them read it back to you, pointing to each word as they read.

If children are adding additional words to the sentence as they read, have them write those words in the correct place within the sentence.

TEKS
1.5C understand that written words are separated by spaces
1.6A demonstrate the concept of word
1.17C use phonological knowledge to write messages
1.17D write messages that move left-to-right and top-to-bottom
1.18C write to record ideas and reflections

Capitalizing First Names

Lesson Background

English language learners often form letters in their names in many different ways, including using all capitals. This is especially true in other languages. Children with different language backgrounds may not capitalize their first or last names, or they may use capital letters for their whole names. This Mini-lesson will be a model for children showing the appropriate way to write people's names in English. Although some children may not be developmentally ready to form lowercase letters, it is important for them to see this model.

Teaching the Lesson

- *Today I want to share a letter by (Fluffy, our hamster). He wrote a letter telling the principal* (show his or her picture if possible) *about the books* (hold up a book or two) *we have been reading in class. As I read the letter to you, I want you to look for your names. (Fluffy) is still learning how to write your names correctly. We'll have to be detectives to see if he did a good job writing your names.*

- Read the letter to children, pausing as you read a child's name. Use a pointer so children can follow along as you read.

- After reading the letter, have children look at the name tags on their desks or distribute name tags if necessary. *Look at your name tags and find your name in the letter that (Fluffy) wrote. Be a good detective and look to see if (Fluffy) wrote your name the correct way, just like on your name tag.* You may want to pick a child and demonstrate first.

- As children become aware of the differences between their name tags and their names in the letter, explain that names of people always begin with capital letters. *Our names are very important to us. In English we write a capital letter at the beginning of a person's name to show how important names are.*

- Have volunteers point to capital letters that you have posted throughout the room. Then have volunteers find names that need to be changed.

Extending the Lesson

Have children come up and practice writing their own names on an easel pad or the board, making sure that they are beginning their names with capital letters.

On Your Own

Options for **STAGES**

① ② Have children in these Stages practice writing their names with capital letters. They may need to copy them.

③ ④ ⑤ Give children in these Stages a list of names and have them rewrite them using capital letters.

You Will Need

✔ children's name tags

✔ paper; one per child

Using an easel pad, write a letter to the principal or another staff member about the books class members are reading or about other classroom activities. When you write your letter, do not capitalize any of the children's names. Note: If you have a class pet or a school mascot, you may wish to write the letter as though the animal wrote it.

Assessment Connection

When looking through children's writing, make a note of those children who are using capital letters for proper names. For those having difficulty, you may wish to pair them with a friend to help them "edit" their writing, looking specifically for proper names that need to be capitalized.

TEKS **1.5G** recognize how readers use capitalization and punctuation
1.17A write own name and other important words
1.17C use phonological knowledge to write messages
1.17D write messages that move left-to-right and top-to-bottom
1.17G use basic capitalization and punctuation
1.18F write in different forms for different purposes

You Will Need

✔ sheet of chart paper

✔ trade books

✔ marker

✔ Write a short sentence on an easel pad, keeping it covered:

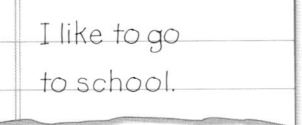

I like to go
to school.

Teacher Tip

Revisit this Mini-lesson often until children show evidence of incorporating the instruction in their writing.

Assessment Connection

Watch for use of the pronoun *I* within children's capitalization usage in their writing.

Lesson Background

You will probably want to teach the Mini-lesson "Capitalizing First Names" on page 43 before you teach this Mini-lesson. English language learners need to recognize that *I* takes the place of their names, and just as their names are capitalized, so is the word *I*.

Teaching the Lesson

- Uncover the sentence you wrote on the easel pad and read it aloud.
- Explain that the word *I* takes the place of the writer's name. Remind children that we capitalize names because they are very important. Just as we capitalize names, we capitalize the word *I* when we write.
- Now have the class say the sentence with you. Ask a volunteer to come to the chart and circle the word *I*.
- Now write a few more sentences that have the word *I* in them. In each case, write a lowercase *i* and ask for volunteers to correct it.

Extending the Lesson

Distribute books and have children look for the word *I* in the text.

On Your Own

Options for STAGES

① ② Have children in these Stages draw pictures of themselves and write the word *I* next to them, making sure it is capitalized.

③ ④ ⑤ Have children in these Stages draw pictures of themselves doing an activity. Then have them write a phrase or sentence to go with the picture, such as *I am walking*. Some children may have to dictate to you. If that is the case, have them try to write and capitalize the word *I*.

TEKS **1.5G** recognize how readers use capitalization and punctuation
1.17G use basic capitalization and punctuation
1.18B write labels, notes, and captions

Mini-lesson 23

Punctuation: Period

Lesson Background

When English language learners begin to write, they often write words or sentences that run on and use no punctuation. They must begin to communicate in their writing where one thought stops and the next begins. This Mini-lesson will introduce the use of a period as a means of telling a reader that a thought (or sentence) has ended. This can be a difficult concept for children.

Teaching the Lesson

- Ask children to close their eyes and picture in their heads where they live. Tell them to imagine that they are going to their friend's house. Have them imagine that they are walking down the street. At the end of the sidewalk, they will see a sign that says *Stop*.
- Have them open their eyes. Show them a picture of a stop sign and use your hand to signal the word *stop*. Ask them what the stop sign means. Explain that, just as they must stop when they get to a street, they must stop when they get to the end of a thought in their writing. *A period is like a stop sign in writing.*

Extending the Lesson

- Tell children you would like them to help you write a few sentences. Choose something relevant, such as an activity you are doing in class. To make things easier, write the first line. Point out the period at the end of your first sentence.
- Then ask for a volunteer to dictate the next line. As you write, model where the periods go for the first few sentences, reinforcing that a period belongs at the end of a thought. Make sure all of your sentences do not end each writing line so that children know that the placement of periods in a text varies. Ask children to tell you when to add periods as they dictate.

On Your Own

Give each child a sentence strip. Ask them to write sentences that tell about something that they like to do. Remind them to end their sentences with a period.

Options for **STAGES**

❷❸ Children in these Stages may dictate a sentence to you. Have those children tell you where the period belongs.	❹❺ Children in these Stages should try to write complete sentences with periods in the correct positions.

You Will Need

- ✔ easel pad
- ✔ markers
- ✔ sentence strips
- ✔ picture of a stop sign

Assessment Connection

Observe what, if any, devices children use to signal the end of a sentence in their writing. Some may make no mark at all; some may always start a new sentence on a new line; some may use a variety of punctuation marks or other symbols interchangeably.

TEKS **1.17G** use basic capitalization and punctuation
1.18A dictate messages
1.21B compose complete sentences and use appropriate end punctuation

Mini-lesson 24
Punctuation: Question Mark

You Will Need

- ✔ brown paper bag
- ✔ school-related object to conceal in bag (pencil, eraser, and so on)
- ✔ easel pad
- ✔ marker
- ✔ journals
- ✔ 2–3 simple questions already written on paper (for Stage 2 children)

Teacher Tip

To make kinesthetic question marks, bend pieces of pipe cleaners and glue each onto a small section of a sentence strip.

Assessment Connection

Listen as children read aloud to see if they understand that the presence of a question mark is a signal to use a questioning voice. Watch for children who are using question marks in their writing.

Lesson Background

To become competent writers, English language learners must understand the correct usage of basic punctuation marks, including question marks. Remember that other languages may use question marks differently. For example, Spanish-language writers write an upside down question mark before the sentence and a "regular" question mark at the end of the sentence.

Teaching the Lesson

- *We're going to play a guessing game. I have something in this paper bag that we use here in the classroom.* Hold up ten fingers. *You can ask me ten questions about it. There's one important rule: I can only answer* yes *or* no. *I'll write your questions and my answers on the chart. When you know what's in the bag yell, "I know!" You'll have one guess.* Record the questions, making a large question mark at the end of each.

- After the tenth question (if a child hasn't already identified the object), have children guess what is in the bag. Then pull the object out of the bag and show it to the class. *Your questions really helped you solve the mystery. Let's look at those questions again.* Point to the question mark at the end of a sentence. *Look at this punctuation mark. Does anyone know what it is called? All of these questions that I wrote end with a question mark. That is how we know that the sentences are* asking *sentences. When you are reading, a question mark at the end of a sentence tells you how to read the sentence. Listen to me read one of your questions. Do you hear how my voice goes up at the end? Now read the question with me.*

Extending the Lesson

Invite children to brainstorm a list of additional questions beginning with words such as *who, what, where, when, why, can,* and *are.* Write these questions on an easel pad.

On Your Own

Options for **STAGES**

② Have children in this Stage fill in the blanks of 2–3 simple sentences and add a question mark at the end. For example, *Can you go to the _____* Students can dictate their word to you. Have them draw the question mark.

③④⑤ Have children in these Stages think of a question they have about school. Then they can write those questions in their journals. Some children may need to dictate their questions to you. After you write them, have children add question marks.

TEKS **1.17G** *use basic capitalization and punctuation*
1.21B *compose complete sentences and use appropriate end punctuation*

Punctuation: Exclamation Point

Lesson Background

English language learners are naturally excited about life and learning. This is evident as we listen to them tell a personal experience story. They can also indicate this excitement in their writing by using the exclamation point. Remember that just like the question mark, other languages may use exclamation points differently. For example, Spanish-language writers write an upside down exclamation point before the sentence as well as a "regular" exclamation point at the end of the sentence.

Teaching the Lesson

Share a familiar Big Book with children. Read sentences ending with exclamation points with obvious excitement. After reading, return to a sentence that features an exclamation point. Reread the sentence. *How does the author tell us that this sentence should be read in an excited voice?* Help children identify the exclamation point at the end of the sentence. Explain that when they see an exclamation point, they should read the sentence with excitement. Read the sentence again, this time using a normal reading voice. Then read the same sentence with excitement. Ask children if they can hear a difference.

Extending the Lesson

Explain that children can use exclamation points when they are writing. Using an exclamation point will tell their readers that the sentence should be read with excitement. Write something exciting such as, "Tomorrow is my birthday!" on an easel pad, ending with a large exclamation point. You may want to draw a picture of a birthday cake next to it. Show children how to make an exclamation point. Ask children for more exciting sentences and write them on the easel pad.

On Your Own

Distribute writing paper to children. Ask them to each draw a picture of something that they think is exciting. If time permits, have volunteers share their drawings and read their sentences—with excitement!

You Will Need

- ✔ familiar Big Book that features exclamation points
- ✔ easel pad
- ✔ marker
- ✔ writing paper

Assessment Connection

Look for exclamation points in children's writing. Ask them to read these sentences aloud when possible. Assess their understanding of the exclamation point by noting whether they read the sentences with the appropriate expression.

Options for **STAGES**

② Have children in this Stage draw a picture and write a word or two, as they are able.

❸❹❺ Have children in these Stages draw a picture and write a phrase or a sentence that ends with an exclamation point. Some children may have to dictate to you. After you write the sentences, have them draw the exclamation points.

TEKS **1.17G** use basic capitalization and punctuation
1.18A dictate messages
1.21B compose complete sentences and use appropriate end punctuation

Mini-lesson 26
Writing About Your Own Drawing

You Will Need

✔ teacher-drawn pictures on an easel pad showing children playing with friends or children participating in sports

✔ black marker

✔ colored markers

✔ crayons

✔ paper

Teacher Tip

Use this Mini-lesson to build on your shared writing lessons whenever the opportunity arises in the classroom.

Assessment Connection

Note children who are reluctant to attempt writing. Have them dictate labels or captions to you. As you write their words, model your thinking process.

Lesson Background

When English language learners first begin writing, most of the writing consists of pictures. One way to begin the transition into writing words is to have them write about their own drawings.

Teaching the Lesson

- Show children the picture you have drawn on the easel pad. Ask questions, such as *What do you see going on in this picture? What are these children doing? What do you think the people are laughing about? What do you think they are talking about?* Accept all answers.
- Choose one of the answers given by children and move to the chalkboard or easel pad. Tell children that not only can you talk about a picture, you can write about it too. When you write about a picture, it tells what you were thinking about when you drew it.
- Write a statement under the picture, modeling directionality, capitalization, and punctuation. Reread the statement aloud to children and ask if they think what you wrote matches the picture.

Extending the Lesson

If you have time, repeat the process with another drawing.

On Your Own

Put a selection of stencils in a writing center, along with a variety of colored markers, crayons, and paper.

Options for STAGES

❷❸ Encourage children in these Stages to draw an object using one of the stencils and to add a few words or a phrase to describe the picture.

❹❺ Encourage children in these Stages to draw an object using one of the stencils and to add a sentence to describe the picture.

Writing About a Picture

Lesson Background

English language learners sometimes have trouble coming up with ideas for their writing. This Mini-lesson helps to "jump start" children's ideas by inviting them to write about real, interesting, action-packed pictures.

Teaching the Lesson

- *I took this picture and want to show it to you.* Point to actions in the picture. *What do you think is happening in this picture? Yes, it looks like the family is laughing and playing. Why do you think they are laughing?* Elicit responses. *This picture helps me remember different things that happened that day, so I can write about them.* Tell about something that happened, referring to the picture.

- Under the picture, write sentences to accompany the action shown, reading aloud as you write, such as:

> My family is playing baseball. They are laughing because my
>
> sister fell into a puddle when she caught the ball.

This is the beginning of my writing. It tells us about what happened that day. Sometimes it helps to look at a picture before I begin to write.

Extending the Lesson

I need help adding to my writing. I can think of different things that happened that day, but I'm not sure what to write about. Tell them some of the things that happened and ask them to help you choose what to write about. *I want to write about what happened before the picture was taken and after the picture was taken. I want to say that we went on a picnic before we played baseball, and after our game my sister had wet shoes all day!*

On Your Own

Using their own photographs or magazine pictures, have children write their own piece. As children work, circulate, helping with ideas as needed. Children may also need to dictate to you. Display completed writing and the pictures that inspired them, or collate the pieces and pictures into a class anthology.

Options for STAGES

❷ Children in this Stage may be able to label their pictures.	❸ Children in this Stage may only be able to write a couple of short phrases.	❹❺ Children in these Stages will work independently on their writing. They should be able to write 2–3 sentences.

You Will Need

Prior to this Mini-lesson, you will need to instruct children to bring in photographs from home that show an event, such as a family celebration or vacation. If children do not have photographs, they can use a picture from a magazine.

You will also need to look through your own photographs that show action and detail—canoeing down a river, a soccer game, a party, and so on, and select one to attach to the top of an easel pad. You may need to enlarge the photograph.

✔ personal photographs depicting action or telling a story
✔ easel pad
✔ markers
✔ paper; one per child

Assessment Connection

As you look through children's writing, be sure that they are describing the actions in their pictures correctly.

TEKS **1.18B** write labels, notes, and captions
1.23B record or dictate own knowledge of a topic in various ways

Mini-lesson 28
Writing from Patterned Text

You Will Need

✔ sample "I can" book (see "Teaching the Lesson")

✔ copies of "I can" book pages; one per child (see below)

✔ 2" x 11" strips of construction paper; two per child; two for sample book

I can _____.
I can _____.
I can _____.
I can _____.
I can _____.

Teacher Tip

Revisit this Mini-lesson often until children show evidence of incorporating the instruction in their writing.

Assessment Connection

Check children's patterned writing to see if they have mastered the concept of changing the words while sticking to the pattern. Invite more capable writers to develop their own ideas for patterns.

Lesson Background

A simple way to get reluctant writers to write is to provide them with patterned text to use. English language learners can quickly produce writing of which they will be proud by merely changing a few words in the pattern.

Teaching the Lesson

- Prepare for the lesson by making a master book page (see margin). You can do this on a computer if you have one available. If you are doing it by hand, draw dashed horizontal lines every two inches down a sheet of 8 1/2" × 11" paper. To make a sample book, cut the five strips apart, complete each sentence with something you can do, and staple the pages together on the left. Use two strips of construction paper to make a cover for the book.

- Share your sample book by reading it aloud to children. After you finish reading, ask children if they can see what is the same on each page. Help them conclude that each page starts with the same phrase *I can*. Explain that your book is called a "pattern book." Only a few words change on each page.

Extending the Lesson

Have children dictate to you things that they can do.

Options for STAGES

❶ Have children in this Stage show you something that they can do.

❷❸❹❺ Have children in these Stages tell you something that they can do.

On Your Own

Tell children that they can write their own *I can* pattern books. Give each child one copy of the book strips to cut apart.

Options for STAGES

❶ Children in this Stage can draw pictures of things they can do, or they can show you what they can do as you write the words in the blanks.

❷❸❹❺ Children in these Stages can try to write what they can do. Some children may have to dictate to you.

Children can illustrate their pages as they fill in the blanks. After children have finished their writing, ask them to put them in order. Then let children choose construction paper strips for covers. Staple the covers and pages together on the left. After children decorate their covers, have them write the title *I can* or write it for them. Ask for volunteers to share their books by reading them aloud or read some of the books aloud to them.

1.18C write to record ideas and reflections
1.24A develop and expand repertoire of learning strategies

Naming Words

Lesson Background

As English language learners begin to write, they need to understand that sentences are made up of different parts of speech. This Mini-lesson will focus on nouns, or naming words. Children will learn that naming words represent people, places, and things.

Teaching the Lesson

- Tell children that naming words, or nouns, are the words in a sentence that stand for people, places, or things. Show children the paper divided into three sections. Explain what each of these words means.
- Read the first word you have written on a separate piece of paper *(girl)* and have children repeat it after you. *Where do you think I should write the word* girl? *Is a girl a person, a place, or a thing?* Elicit responses. *That's right, a girl is a person.* Write *girl* under the column titled Person.
- Do the same thing with the rest of the words on your list, discussing each word and showing pictures of the words, if possible.

Extending the Lesson

Choose one or two words from each column and write sentences using them. Go back and circle the people with a red marker, the places with a green marker, and the things with a blue marker.

On Your Own

Options for STAGES ◉ ◎ ◉ ◎ ◉ ◎ ◉ ◎ ◉ ◉

❸ Put children in this Stage in pairs. Give each pair a list of simple naming words with pictures next to them and a smaller version of the chart. Have them write the words in the correct columns. Walk around the room and assist children if necessary.

❹❺ Have children in these Stages independently write four to five sentences using some of the words you have discussed or their own words. Have them circle the naming words using the same colored markers you used in "Extending the Lesson."

You Will Need

- ✔ easel pad paper divided into three sections (see below)
- ✔ marker
- ✔ list of naming words (for Stage 3)
- ✔ paper; one per student
- ✔ a list of words written on a separate piece of paper including words such as: *girl, boy, Mexico, China, pencil, tortilla, rice, Mom, Dad, water, bowl, brother,* and so on
- ✔ a picture of each item you will be discussing (if possible)
- ✔ three different colored markers

Person	Place	Thing

Assessment Connection

As you are looking through their work, check to see if children understand the difference between people, places, and things. If not, during an individual conference, go over the difference between the three types of naming words.

 TEKS **1.11C** identify words that name persons, places, or things and words that name actions
1.21A use nouns and verbs in sentences

Mini-lesson 30
Writing a How-to

You Will Need

✔ envelopes

✔ spider directions (below)

✔ blank copy paper; one sheet per child

✔ finished spider

✔ patterns for spider body and legs

✔ black construction paper and scraps of yellow construction paper

✔ scissors and glue

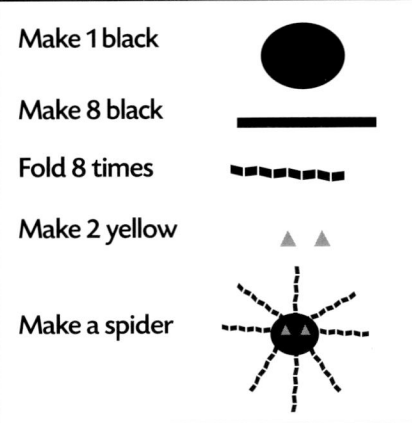

Make 1 black

Make 8 black

Fold 8 times

Make 2 yellow

Make a spider

Teacher Tip

Tailor your Mini-lesson to different Stages of English Language Acquisition and to the needs of the children in your classroom.

Assessment Connection

As children use and write how-to directions, note their ability to follow or create a logical sequence of steps.

TEKS 1.18E write to communicate with a variety of audiences
1.18F write in different forms for different purposes

Lesson Background

English language learners feel special when they know how to do something and feel even better when they are asked to show someone else what they know. They should know that a "how-to" is a specific kind of writing, and they should be encouraged to begin reading and writing in this unique format.

Teaching the Lesson

- Before teaching the lesson, make a copy of the directions for each child, leaving space between each step. Cut apart the directions and place them in individual envelopes. Set up a center with patterns and materials for making spiders.
- Explain to children that when someone knows how to do something, he or she can help others learn to do the same thing by writing "how-to" directions. Explain that directions need to be written very carefully and in order. Discuss with children what might happen if directions are not complete or steps for doing something are not in the correct order.
- Tell children that they are going to be making spiders and display a finished sample. Explain that they will also be making "how-to" directions. Distribute envelopes and copy paper. *The how-to directions I wrote are not in order. So we need to figure out which step comes first and what to do after that.*
- Have children look at the direction strips and discuss a logical order for making a spider. The order does not matter for some of the directions—making the eyes before the legs, or vice versa—but for most of the directions the order is important.

Extending the Lesson

Invite children to think of other activities that would need "how-to" directions.

On Your Own

Have children arrange the directions in order on their desks. Go from child to child, checking to see that each has a workable sequence. If you have time, let children share their directions and spiders with the class.

Options for **STAGES**

① ② Have children in these Stages put the strips in order. You may need to have them look at directions glued onto paper in the correct order so they can match their order to the model. After they put the strips in order, have them glue them onto the paper and then have them make the spiders.

③ ④ ⑤ Have children in these Stages put the strips in order and explain the reasoning behind the order to a partner. Then have them make the spiders.

Prewriting Activities

Lesson Background

Because of language limitations, English language learners often have difficulty knowing how to approach the writing process. We can empower them by providing different strategies to help them get organized before they begin writing. In this Mini-lesson, we will be showing children three different ways to get organized:

• with a picture
• with a list
• with a cluster diagram

Teaching the Lesson

• *I want to write about how to cook rice, but I don't know where to begin.* Show the drawing of all of the items. *One thing I can do is draw a picture of all of the things I will need to cook rice.* Name all of the different items, pointing to each as you say it.

• *Another thing that I can do is write out a list of all of the things I will need.* Have children tell you what you need and write the items in list form on the easel pad.

• *One more thing I can do is use this.* Show the graphic organizer. *This is called a graphic organizer. It helps me put things in order. In each box, I can draw a picture of what I need to do to make rice.* Draw a picture in each box explaining the steps you are going to take to make rice. *Then under each box, I can write a few words or a sentence about the picture.* Invite children to suggest a few words to write under each box. *These are all different things that I can do to help me get ready to write. It is very important that you choose one of these things to do each time you would like to write something.*

Extending the Lesson

Choose one of the prewriting activities you have just modeled and use it to write about how to cook rice.

On Your Own

Give children a topic to write about or let them choose one of their own.

Options for STAGES

❸ Put children in this Stage in pairs and have them draw a picture or make a list to do their prewriting activity.

❹❺ Have children in these Stages work independently using the graphic organizer to do their prewriting activity.

You Will Need

✔ a drawing of a pot, some water in a measuring cup, some uncooked rice, and a stove
✔ easel pad to make a list
✔ a blank graphic organizer (such as the shared writing card in Unit 5)
✔ graphic organizers; one per child
✔ paper; one per child

Assessment Connection

To ensure that children are using one of the prewriting activities, have them show it to you. This will enable you to help them clarify their steps before they begin writing.

TEKS **1.18F** write in different forms for different purposes
1.19A generate ideas before writing on self-selected topics
1.19B generate ideas before writing on assigned tasks
1.23B record or dictate own knowledge of a topic in various ways
1.24A develop and expand repertoire of learning strategies

Mini-lesson 32
Action Words

You Will Need

- ✔ easel pad
- ✔ marker
- ✔ paper
- ✔ familiar Big Books (for Stages 4–5)
- ✔ the following sentence written on an easel pad:

> When I am at home,
> I like to _____

Lesson Background

It is important for English language learners to have a great deal of experience with action words. It is important to explain that an action word means that someone is *doing* something. Once children are familiar with the use of action words, introduce the term *verb*.

Teaching the Lesson

- Pick a child to walk around the room. *Who can tell me what (Ivan) is doing? That's right, (Ivan) is walking. When someone is doing something it is called an action.* Write the sentence *(Ivan) is walking* on an easel pad, circle the word *walking* and read the sentence aloud. *Walking is the action word because it tells what (Ivan) is doing.*
- Show children the sentence you have written and read it aloud. *Who can help me fill in the blank?* Elicit responses such as: *read, eat, play,* and so on, and write them under the blank. Tell children that these are all action words.

Extending the Lesson

Write a few more sentences that include action words and have children help you decide what those words are. Encourage children to use a dictionary to find synonyms for action words. Remind children to use alphabetical order when looking up words.

On Your Own

Assessment Connection

When conferencing with children, pick a sentence out of their writing that includes an action word and have them point it out to you.

Options for **STAGES**		
❷ Have children in this Stage draw pictures of themselves doing something and then choose one of the following: dictate to you what they are doing, write one or two words about their action, or write about their action in their home language.	❸ Have children in this Stage draw pictures of themselves doing something, write a phrase or sentence about what they are doing, and circle the action word.	❹❺ Have children in these Stages look through familiar Big Books and pick out two or three sentences that have action words in them, write them down, and circle the action words.

TEKS **1.11C** identify words that name persons, places, or things and words that name actions
1.15D use alphabetical order to locate information
1.18A dictate messages
1.18C write to record ideas and reflections
1.20D use resources to find correct spellings, synonyms, and replacement words
1.21A use nouns and verbs in sentences
1.24C monitor language production and employ self-corrective techniques

Describing Words

Lesson Background

Through read-alouds, English language learners hear descriptive language but have not yet made the transition to using it in their own writing. This Mini-lesson will begin calling children's attention to the use of descriptive words in their writing.

Teaching the Lesson

- Read your descriptive paragraph to children. As you read, be sure to emphasize the descriptive words. Ask them to tell you about the sweater, using prompts such as, *What color is it? Is it big or small? When do I wear it? We know what my sweater looks like because of the describing words,* big, red, *and* warm; *and we know that I wear my sweater on* cold, snowy *days.*

- Have children help you circle the describing words. After the words are circled, talk about how important it is for authors to use these kinds of words because they help readers picture things in their heads and make the sentences more interesting.

Extending the Lesson

Write a sentence leaving a blank where a describing word will go, such as *The _____ ball was rolling down the hill.* You may even want to show children a ball to help them. Then have children think of words to write in the blank, such as *big, round, shiny, red,* and so on.

On Your Own

Options for STAGES

❷ ❸ Put children in these Stages in pairs mixing Stage 2 and 3 children. Give each pair a simple picture from a magazine and have them write describing words or phrases for the picture.

❹ ❺ Have children in these Stages draw a picture and write a descriptive sentence to go with it.

You Will Need

✔ On an easel pad, write a short paragraph describing something. Use many descriptive words, for example, *Today I am wearing my favorite red sweater. I love my big, warm sweater because it keeps me warm on cold, snowy days.*

✔ magazine pictures that are colorful and show action

✔ paper

Assessment Connection

English language learners may find it difficult to use a variety of descriptive words until they have an adequate vocabulary. If they are having trouble, use the following activity to help them increase their range of descriptive words. On the board, list different categories of nouns, such as *animals, people, toys,* and so on. In a small group, ask children to think of describing words to go with the nouns.

TEKS **1.18C** write to record ideas and reflections

Mini-lesson 34
Contractions

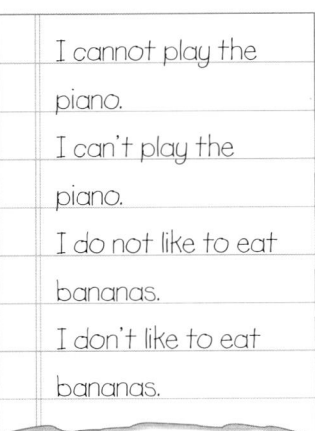

Lesson Background

When we speak, we often combine certain words. These combined words are called *contractions*. English language learners need to understand that any word they speak can also be written. This includes contractions.

Teaching the Lesson

- Explain to children that sometimes we can say two words more easily and quickly if we make them one word. *I can say I* do not *want to go to bed or I* don't *want to go to bed. When I put the two words together, I can say them faster.* Tell children that when they combine two words into one, they are making a *contraction*.
- Read aloud the sentences you have written. Guide children to see that the second sentence in each set means exactly the same as the first, but you used a contraction to write it.
- Write the contractions below on an easel pad, modeling how and where to write each apostrophe. Say each word as you write it. Point to the apostrophe in the word *can't*. *I can make two words a contraction when I put an apostrophe where the missing letters go.* cannot = can't   do not = don't   is not = isn't

Extending the Lesson

- Using a nonfiction Big Book with which the children are familiar, choose a page that contains one or more of the contractions above. Read the page with children. *Do you see any contractions on this page?* Ask volunteers to point to the contractions. You may also want to place sticky notes by each one as it is located.
- You may wish to write the contractions from this lesson on a poster to hang on the wall for future reference and add to it as children learn new contractions.

On Your Own

Divide the class into three groups. Assign each group one of the sets of contractions from above. Ask them to spend a few minutes practicing the contractions, saying them first and then writing them. Circulate around the room to be sure children are marking the apostrophe in the correct place.

Options for **STAGES**

❸ Put children in this Stage in pairs and have them find contractions in a Big Book. Ask them to write the sentences that contain those contractions.

❹❺ Children in these Stages can create new sentences using contractions they have learned. Once they are finished they can read their sentences to a friend.

Reading Your Work to Yourself

Lesson Background

Many times when English language learners finish a piece of writing, they want to share it right away, or they put it away saying, "I'm done." Often they do not reread their writing before doing this. It is essential, however, to help them understand the importance of rereading their work. We want children to be proud of their writing. By rereading writers make sure they are happy with the piece before sharing it or putting it away.

Teaching the Lesson

- *I am so excited! I just finished writing about my picture.* Point to the picture. *It is about a trip that I took. I want to read it to you, but I want to make sure that I didn't forget anything.*

- Point to yourself. *I should read it to myself first.* Read your writing aloud, as if you were reading to yourself. *I like my writing about my trip, and the picture of the airplane tells you how I went there. I think I'm done. But wait a minute! I didn't say where I went. I'd better include that. That's an important part. How would the people who read my writing know where I went unless I write it?* Add to your writing. *OK, I think I'm done. I'm going to read it to myself again, and then I'll share it with a friend.*

- Read your writing aloud again, as if you were reading to yourself. *Now anyone who reads about my trip will know where I went. I like my new writing much better.*

Extending the Lesson

If there is time, add even more to your writing, getting ideas from children as you write.

On Your Own

When you are done with your writing today, reread your work and ask yourself questions. "Am I really done? Do I like my writing? What else could I write about? Will my friends understand what I wrote?" When you are really done, share your writing with a friend.

Options for STAGES

| ❸ Ask children in this Stage the questions you have modeled. Then have them share their writing with each other. | ❹❺ Remind children in these Stages to ask themselves the questions you have modeled. Then have them share their writing with each other. |

You Will Need

✔ a piece of writing on an easel pad

✔ marker

Draw a picture and write a few sentences about it, leaving out details. Example: *I went on a trip. It was fun. We went on an airplane.*

Assessment Connection

If some children seem to hurry through their writing, work with them individually, asking them the questions they should begin to ask themselves.

TEKS 1.18E write to communicate with a variety of audiences
1.22C determine how own writing achieves its purposes

Mini-lesson 36
Reading to a Peer or Group

Lesson Background

Sharing their writing with peers, either individually or as a group, is something new for most English language learners. This Mini-lesson will help them understand why writers read their work to peers and how they should act as readers and as listeners.

Teaching the Lesson

- Show children a book and point to your ear. *How many of you like to listen to stories? So do I! Did you know that many of the authors of the books we have read shared their work with someone before it was finished? Why do you think writers like to show someone else what they wrote?* Accept all responses. *Yes, those are all good reasons.*

- *Reading what you wrote to a friend or someone in your family is a good way to find out if it makes sense. I want you to think about how you should read your work to someone else. Let's make a list that tells us how a writer should act when sharing his or her work.*

- Help children come up with ideas such as reading in a loud, clear voice; using expression; sitting up straight while reading; showing illustrations to the listeners; and so on. *Those are wonderful ideas. We can keep them in mind when we read our writing to someone.*

Teacher Tip

Always model for children before letting them work on their own.

Extending the Lesson

Demonstrate how to read your work to the class.

On Your Own

Hold up a child's journal. *Now I'd like each of you to find a page in your journal that you would like to share with a partner. Make sure you think about how to make the reading enjoyable for the person who is listening. The listener should make sure that he or she is paying attention.*

Assessment Connection

Observe children's behavior as they read to their peers and listen to the writing of others. Note which children are good oral presenters and which children will need more coaching.

Options for **STAGES**

❶ Have children in this Stage share their pictures with each other. Pair children who have the same home language so that they can talk about the pictures when possible.

❷❸❹❺ Have children in these Stages take turns sharing what they have drawn or reading what they have written.

TEKS 1.18E write to communicate with a variety of audiences
1.24C monitor language production and employ self-corrective techniques

Mini-lesson 37
Asking for Comments

Lesson Background

"Watch me!" is one way young English language learners constantly seek feedback from adults and other children. "Listen to what I wrote!" is another way for them to seek valuable feedback from others. This Mini-lesson will help them understand how asking for comments from peers can help to shape their writing.

Teaching the Lesson

- *I have something that I just wrote. I wonder if you would like to help me with it. I want to read my writing to you. Then I would like you to tell me what you think about it. You might think it should be longer, or you might want me to take something out. I am really interested in hearing what you think. I hope you can help me make my writing better. I will sit in the author's chair while I read. I will also use a voice that you all can hear. Make sure you are being good listeners by thinking about what you are hearing.*

- Read your writing aloud, modeling showing pictures, using a clear voice, making eye contact with your listeners, and so on. *That's my writing. Who would like to make a comment?*

- Make sure to explain to children that they should only be making positive comments and not saying things such as "I don't like it" or "You're a bad writer." Model a helpful comment, such as *I liked your story! Try adding more describing words.* Take a few moments to listen to children's comments. Respond to each with comments, such as *That's a good idea, I'll think about doing that,* or *I can see I need to make that clearer so you'll understand.* Thank children for helping you and explain that you will keep their comments in mind as you continue to work on your writing. *It was fun to read my writing to you and hear what you think.*

Extending the Lesson

If there is time, choose another piece of your writing and get comments from children.

On Your Own

Arrange children in pairs. *Now I'd like you to read something you have written to a friend and have him or her comment. Then you can trade places, so everyone will get a chance to read. Be sure your comments are helpful, like they were for me. After it is your turn to read, ask for a comment or two about the writing.* Circulate, offering encouragement as needed.

Options for **STAGES**

❸ Have children in this Stage give comments to each other orally.	❹❺ Have children in these Stages write comments to each other.

You Will Need

- ✔ something you have written
- ✔ author's chair
- ✔ children's journals or writing samples

Assessment Connection

Notice how children act as they share their own writing and make comments about someone else's writing. Some children may find it difficult to read aloud to a peer. Others may find it difficult to accept suggestions for improvement. Offer guidance and support as needed.

 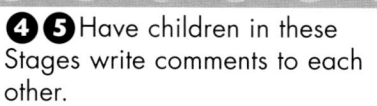 **1.22B** respond constructively to others' writing
1.24G use accessible language and learn new and essential language

Mini-lesson 38
Conferencing with the Teacher

You Will Need
✔ children's writing in progress

Lesson Background

A conference is a one-on-one conversation between a child and the teacher about the purpose and content of the child's writing. It is a time for assessing the child's progress and making anecdotal notes for evaluation. You may also wish to use the Writing Rubric for English Language Writers on pages 18–19.

Teaching the Lesson

We have been talking about writing. Hold up a child's journal. *You all have written and drawn pictures in your journals and for other kinds of writing. Now each of you will have a turn to talk to me about your writing and drawings. This is called a conference. It is a special meeting between a writer and a teacher. I will meet with each of you, one at a time. I will ask you to read or show me something that's in your journal. If you can, you will read it to me. Then we will talk about it. I will probably ask you some questions, and then you can ask me some questions. You can also tell me about a part that was difficult to do.*

Teacher Tip

Tailor the Mini-lesson to different Stages of English Language Acquisition and to the needs of the children in your classroom.

Extending the Lesson

Have children choose another example of their writing (or drawing) that they would like to share with you. If possible, children can tell you about a part that was difficult to do.

On Your Own

Look in your journal or writing portfolio now and pick out a page that you want to share in your conference with me. It can be something that's finished or something that you're working on. Look at it before we meet, so you can decide if you have any questions for me. Some of you will meet with me today, and some of you will meet with me a different day.

Assessment Connection

Information obtained during a conference can provide the teacher with teaching points to be addressed during modeled writing the following day.

Options for **STAGES**

❶❷ Children in these Stages may only be able to share a picture or a few words with you.

❸❹❺ As you conference with children in these Stages, use prompts such as "Tell me about this picture," "How does this picture go with your writing?" and "What was the hardest thing about writing this?"

TEKS **1.22A** identify the most effective features of a piece of writing
1.24C monitor language production and employ self-corrective techniques

Editing Home Language Usage

Lesson Background

As English language learners begin to write, they may not have an extensive English vocabulary. As they write, they may substitute words from their home languages for English words. For example, they may write *I have a nice reloj* (pronounced *ray-LOH*) because they do not know the word for *watch* in English. In this Mini-lesson you will be showing children how to go back to their writing and edit their home language usage. It is important to let children know that, as they are writing their first drafts in English, it is acceptable to fall back on their home languages when they are focusing on getting their meaning across.

Teaching the Lesson

- *I am going to show you a sentence that I wrote a month ago.* Read the sentence aloud. *Does anyone notice that I used the word* rojo *(pronounced ROH-hoh)? Does that sound like an English word? No, it is a Spanish word. When I read my sentence out loud, it helps me hear the words I need to fix.* (Choose a native English speaker in your classroom.) *I have to think about how (Susan) would say it. (Susan) would say* red, *not* rojo. *I have to cross out* rojo *and write* red. *Now I have edited my sentence.*

- *When you write your first draft, it is OK to write things in your home language. That is why it is important that you edit your papers. You need to read your work out loud to yourself or a friend and think about what words you wrote in your home language that need to be written in English. Always think about how (Susan) or (Richard) might say something.*

Extending the Lesson

Choose a familiar word, either in Spanish or another language, and write it in a sentence. Ask children to figure out the word in English and edit the sentence.

On Your Own

Have children look back at two or three pieces of writing to see if they need to fix any words that were written in their home language. If home language use is not an issue for a child, he or she can help a buddy.

Options for **STAGES**

❷❸ Choose a piece of writing for children in these Stages that includes home language words. Have children try to locate and edit them.

❹❺ Have children in these Stages choose and edit a selection of their own work for home language usage.

You Will Need

✔ the following sentence written on an easel pad:

> My mother drives a
> rojo car.

✔ marker

Assessment Connection

As you are looking at first drafts and final drafts, check to see that children are editing their home language usage. If not, during a conference, you may want to ask children if they notice any words that need to be changed to English and help them decide what to do.

TEKS **1.19D** revise selected drafts for varied purposes
1.24C monitor language production and employ self-corrective techniques

Mini-lesson 40
Using Academic Words

Lesson Background

As English language learners are writing, they often forget to use words they have learned in school. These words are called academic words. This Mini-lesson will show children how to look back in their writing and find words that they can substitute with academic words.

Teaching the Lesson

As you know, we have been studying plants. I have written a few sentences that I would like to show you. Read the sentences aloud. *These are nice sentences that I wrote, but I think I can make them better. That is called editing. Let's look at the first sentence again.* Reread the first sentence. *What word that we have been talking about in class can I use instead of* dirt? Elicit and validate responses. *That is right, I can use the word* soil *instead of* dirt. Soil *is a school word. It is important that when I am writing, I try to use a school word whenever I can. When I am editing I will ask myself, "Can I use one of the words I have been using in class?"*

Extending the Lesson

Extend the lesson using another sentence. For example: *I live in a nice place.* Instead of the word *place,* use the word *apartment* or *house.* As you introduce new academic words, write them on a chart to be displayed for children to use as a writing tool. If possible, illustrate the words. Encourage children to use a dictionary or thesaurus to find replacement words and synonyms. Remind children to use alphabetical order when looking up words.

On Your Own

Options for STAGES

❷❸ Choose a piece of writing (labels, phrases, or sentences) that children in these Stages have written in which an academic word can be substituted for a word they have used. Have them edit their work using academic words.

❹❺ Have children in these stages choose one or two pieces of their own writing and look for words that can be substituted with academic words.

TEKS
1.10B use graphs, charts, signs, captions, and other informational texts to acquire information
1.15D use alphabetical order to locate information
1.19D revise selected drafts for varied purposes
1.20D use resources to find correct spellings, synonyms, and replacement words
1.24F make connections across content areas and use language and concepts in different ways

Adding Interesting Words

Lesson Background

English language learners use simple sentences when they begin to write. Often their speaking vocabulary is much more developed than their writing vocabulary. You can show them how to add interesting words to expand their writing and make it more interesting.

Teaching the Lesson

- *Today we are going to learn to add some interesting words to our writing. On this paper, there is a sentence that has a blank and a picture. First let's read the sentence without the blank.* We saw a tiger at the zoo. *Does that tell you a lot about the tiger? No, it doesn't. We need some interesting words that tell about this tiger. Have any of you seen a tiger at the zoo or on television? I remember seeing a tiger. He was huge. Let's think of more words to describe a tiger. I will write your ideas under the blank, and we can decide which one we want to use.*

We saw a _____ at the zoo.
huge
furry
loud
hungry
big
mean

- Record words under the blanks as shown. Reread the sentence together using each of the new words in the sentence. Then vote on which one the class likes the best. *When we add words like these to our sentence, it makes it much more interesting. Remember that you don't have to use only one interesting word at a time. For example, you could say* We saw a big, mean lion at the zoo.

Extending the Lesson

- Create a list of interesting words to post in your classroom.

On Our Own

Let's think of other animals we've seen. Write a list of animals on the board. *When you write in your journal today, choose an animal that you would like to write about. Use interesting words to describe the animal. Try to choose a different animal than the person sitting next to you. Then you can draw a picture of your animal to go with your writing.*

Options for STAGES

❸ Have children in this Stage write a few words or a phrase about an animal.

❹❺ Have children in these Stages write 2–3 sentences about an animal.

You Will Need

- ✔ easel pad with cloze activity already prepared
- ✔ marker
- ✔ student journals

Assessment Connection

Conduct individual conferences and ask children what interesting words they are using to describe their animals.

TEKS **1.19B** generate ideas before writing on assigned tasks
1.19D revise selected drafts for varied purposes

Mini-lesson 42
Using a Variety of Sentence Patterns

You Will Need

✔ easel pad

✔ marker

✔ student journals

✔ a paragraph written on an easel pad (see "Teaching the Lesson")

✔ simple sentence written on 8½" x 11" paper (for children in Stage 3)

Teacher Tip

Revisit this Mini-lesson often until children show evidence of incorporating the instruction in their writing.

Assessment Connection

Watch for use of the word *and* to combine simple sentences. If children are still writing simple sentences, sit down with them and go over their writing. Ask how they can make their sentences more interesting.

Lesson Background

Often English language learners will repeat the same sentence pattern as they write. For example, they may write *I go to the store. I go to the restaurant.* One way that you can show them how to vary their sentences is by joining two sentences with the word *and* such as *I go to the store* and *I go to the restaurant.* After you introduce this idea, make sure to tell children that they should not use *and* all of the time because interesting writing contains a variety of sentences. You might want to explain that *variety* means *lots of different kinds.*

Teaching the Lesson

• Tell children that you have written about what you do when you go to the store. Read the sentences aloud, telling children that they may join in.

> I go to the store. I get a cart. I buy apples. I buy bread. I buy cheese. I buy candy. I go home.

Well, this definitely tells what I do when I go to the store. What do you notice about each sentence?

• Guide children to see that each sentence begins with the word *I* and follows the same pattern. *One way I can make this more interesting is by using the word* and. *Instead of writing* I buy apples, I buy candy, *I can write* I buy apples, and I buy candy *or* I buy apples and candy. *This changes the writing and makes some of the sentences longer and more interesting.*

Extending the Lesson

Have a child tell you about a place that he or she went and write down the sentences as in the example above. As a class, decide which sentences can be combined with the word *and.*

On Your Own

Options for STAGES

❸ Give children in this Stage some simple sentences already written. Have them use the word *and* to combine two or three.

❹❺ Have children in these Stages write their own sentences. Remind them to use the word *and* to make their sentences more interesting.

TEKS **1.19D** revise selected drafts for varied purposes
1.21B compose complete sentences and use appropriate end punctuation

Focusing on Meaning

Lesson Background

As English language learners are beginning to write, they often have trouble getting started. Let children know that they don't need to get hung up on writing their ideas down perfectly the first time. They just need to get their ideas across. They can go back later and edit.

Teaching the Lesson

- *I want to write about my five senses. As I am writing, I won't worry about grammar, punctuation, spelling, and so on. I will just be sure that I write my ideas about my five senses.*
- *Write the following thoughts on an easel pad:*

> You can here with ears You can see with eyes. I touch hands.
>
> A tong I taste with. I can smell flower with nose.

- *As you can see, my English is not perfect. I have forgotten some punctuation, and my spelling isn't all correct. However, in my writing, all I talked about were my five senses. It is important when you are writing a first draft that you do not worry about writing things perfectly the first time. Now that I am done, I can go back and edit it.*

Extending the Lesson

As a class, write a nonfiction piece about something you have done together, such as a field trip, a fire drill, and so on. Write the words down exactly as children say them. Encourage children to write down their ideas and go back to edit their writing after they finish.

On Your Own

Options for **STAGES**

❸ Have children in this Stage write a phrase or sentence about something they have done and edit their work when they finish.

❹❺ Have children in these Stages write several sentences about something they have done and edit their work when they finish.

You Will Need

- ✔ easel pad
- ✔ marker
- ✔ writing paper; one per student

Assessment Connection

While looking at children's writing, make sure that their writing conveys a message, even if there are a lot of errors. Encourage them to work on their errors once the meaning is in place.

 TEKS **1.18C** write to record ideas and reflections
1.18E write to communicate with a variety of audiences
1.19C develop drafts
1.19D revise selected drafts for varied purposes

Mini-lesson 44
Proofreading Symbols: Caret

Lesson Background

As we encourage English language learners to reread their writing, they may discover they have left something out. Instead of having to start over, the writer can use a caret mark to insert what is missing. Keep in mind that English language learners may not realize that they have left out words.

Teaching the Lesson

- *After writers are finished with their writing, they reread what they wrote to be sure it makes sense. Writers use special marks to fix their writing when they find a mistake, so they do not have to rewrite everything.*
- Write the following sentence on an easel pad: *Maria went school today.* Read the sentence aloud and ask children if they think something is missing. (the word *to*)
- Tell children that a special mark called a *caret* is used to show that something needs to be added. Explain that this caret is different from the carrot you eat, but they can remember the symbol because it looks like an upside-down carrot.
- Use an orange crayon or marker to write the symbol for the caret on the easel pad where the missing word should be inserted. Then write the word *to* above the caret.

Extending the Lesson

Flip the easel pad to the next page and write a few simple sentences, leaving out a word in each. Have children fix the sentences with you.

Options for **STAGES**

❸ Have children in this Stage point to where the missing word should go.

❹❺ Have children in these Stages point to where the missing word should go and either write it themselves or dictate it to you.

On Your Own

Remind children as they write in their journals to reread their writing. If they have left out any words or ideas, encourage them to draw a caret and write in the missing words.

TEKS **1.19D** revise selected drafts for varied purposes
1.21B compose complete sentences and use appropriate end punctuation
1.24C monitor language production and employ self-corrective techniques

Proofreading Symbols: Delete Line

Lesson Background
Even beginning writers can learn how to review and revise their writing. This Mini-lesson shows children how to mark words or sentences they want to delete. Keep in mind that English language learners may not realize when they need to delete a word or sentence.

Teaching the Lesson
- *Last night I wrote in my journal about my new car. Today I am going to look at my writing again and see if there's anything that I want to change. I would like you to help me.* Display your writing. Read the writing aloud, inviting children to join in.

> I have a new car. My car is red.
>
> It can go go fast. I drove my car to school today.

- *There is a mistake in this writing. Does anyone see it? Yes, I wrote the word* go *twice. I want to take one* go *out of my writing. But I can't erase because I wrote with marker. Does anyone have an idea about what I can do so I'll remember to take out the extra word when I write my final draft?* Accept all responses. *Those are all good ideas.*
- *When writers check their writing, they have a special way to show which words or sentences don't belong. Instead of erasing, they draw lines through the parts they want to take out. These lines are called* delete marks. Demonstrate drawing a line through the word *go.* *Let's read my writing again. There, that sounds much better. When I copy this writing, I will leave out, or delete, the word I drew a line through.* You may want to demonstrate this.

Extending the Lesson
Write a few more sentences on the easel pad that include mistakes. Ask for volunteers to come up and put the delete mark through the word that does not belong.

On Your Own

Options for STAGES

❸ Give children in this Stage the simple sentences you have prepared. Have them find the mistakes and use the delete mark to edit.

❹❺ Have children in these Stages write two sentences that have mistakes in them. Then they can switch papers with partners and use the delete line to edit each other's mistakes.

You Will Need
- ✔ teacher journal or easel pad with a short nonfiction piece recorded (see "Teaching the Lesson")
- ✔ marker
- ✔ 2 simple sentences containing words that do not belong, written on 8½" x 11" paper (for Stage 3)
- ✔ children's journals or writings in progress

Assessment Connection
Look through children's writing to assess whether or not they are using the delete mark. If some children are doing a lot of messy erasing, review this Mini-lesson with them.

TEKS 1.19C develop drafts
1.19D revise selected drafts for varied purposes
1.24C monitor language production and employ self-corrective techniques

Mini-lesson 46
Checking Punctuation: Period

You Will Need

✔ nonfiction piece written on an easel pad (see "Teaching the Lesson")

✔ markers (two different colors; one for writing and one for punctuation)

✔ journals

Teacher Tip

Revisit this Mini-lesson often until children show evidence of incorporating the instruction in their writing.

Assessment Connection

Look through children's writing portfolios to see if they are using periods consistently. Work one-on-one with children who are having problems, helping them add periods to a piece of writing. Let them use a colored marker to make the punctuation stand out.

 TEKS
1.17G use basic capitalization and punctuation
1.19C develop drafts
1.19D revise selected drafts for varied purposes
1.21B compose complete sentences and use appropriate end punctuation
1.24C monitor language production and employ self-corrective techniques

Lesson Background

Checking end punctuation is an important part of proofreading and one of the first proofing skills that English language learners can master. This Mini-lesson stresses the importance of checking to be sure that statements end with periods.

Teaching the Lesson

• *Here's something I wrote about my garden. I will read it to you. Then I want you to help me check my writing to see if I need to make any changes.* Read the writing aloud, without pausing between sentences.

> My garden is very big I am growing beans and carrots Every day
>
> I pull out the weeds Soon I will have beans and carrots to eat

• *Reading that story made me out of breath! I wonder why that is.* Wait for any responses from children. *You're right! I read it without stopping. Why do you think I did that? Yes, I forgot to put a period at the end of each sentence. Periods would have told me to stop for a second. Can you help me put periods where they belong?* Have children help you add periods to the end of each sentence, using a different-colored marker. *Now I will read my writing again.*

• Reread the sentences, pausing obviously at each period. *That's much better. I needed a period at the end of each sentence so my writing made sense.* Remind children that periods do not go at the end of each line; they go at the end of a thought or sentence.

Extending the Lesson

Show children another piece of writing without punctuation and have them decide where to put the periods.

On Your Own

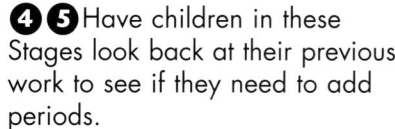

Options for STAGES

❸ Have children in this Stage write 1–2 phrases or sentences, making sure that they insert periods. Some children may need to dictate to you. If children are dictating to you, have them make the period.

❹❺ Have children in these Stages look back at their previous work to see if they need to add periods.

Checking Sequence

Lesson Background

Logical sequencing can be a problem for English language learners. Often a new idea may occur to the writers as they reach the end of their writing. So in it goes, whether it makes sense there or not! This Mini-lesson will help children learn to evaluate the sequence of their own writing. You may want to review the Mini-lesson "Focusing on Meaning" on page 65 before doing this lesson.

Teaching the Lesson

- To prepare for the lesson, write a piece about getting dressed on either index cards or larger paper (see margin). Add drawings to the cards. Tack the cards to a bulletin board or tape the cards to an easel pad, as you read each sentence aloud. Mix up the fifth and sixth card as you display the cards and share the sentences. *That didn't make sense! What did I do wrong? Oh, I put the ending of the story in the middle. I said that I go to school before I put on my shoes. That isn't right. I have to put my shoes on before I go to school.*

- Switch the order of the mixed-up cards. *My writing doesn't make sense if things aren't in order, does it? That is why writers always check their writing to make sure that they have a beginning, a middle, and an end. Which card tells about the beginning of the story? Let's mark that card with a yellow marker.* Use the yellow marker to underline the words on the first card. *Which card tells about the ending? Let's mark that one with a blue marker. That means that the rest of the cards show what happens in the middle. Let's mark with green on all of those cards.*

Extending the Lesson

Options for **STAGES**

❷ For children in this Stage, the same activity can be completed using pictures.

❸ ❹ ❺ For children in these Stages, do the same activity but use a different story.

On Your Own

Put children into groups of three or four. Give each group either three or six cards, depending on the readiness of the group.

Options for **STAGES**

❷ ❸ Have children in these Stages draw pictures for a process. You may want to brainstorm some ideas first. Then have them underline the beginning of the story with a yellow crayon, the middle with green, and the ending with blue.

❹ ❺ Have children in these Stages write a process using the ideas from above. Then have them underline the beginning, middle, and end of the story. They also can draw pictures to go with the cards.

You Will Need
- ✔ writing cards (as shown below)
- ✔ markers (yellow, green, and blue)
- ✔ writing paper; one per student
- ✔ crayons
- ✔ pencils; one per student

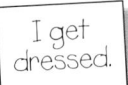  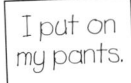

Assessment Connection

When conferencing with children, ask them to identify the three parts of their writing. Children in Stage 2 may only be able to show you the pictures in order.

TEKS **1.12C** retell or act out the order of important events in stories
1.18F write in different forms for different purposes
1.19C develop drafts

Mini-lesson 48
Using Writing Resources

You Will Need

- ✔ picture dictionary (store-bought or handmade)
- ✔ word wall
- ✔ easel pad
- ✔ marker
- ✔ children's writing (for Stages 4–5)

Lesson Background

As English language learners are beginning to write, they will often want to know how to spell different words. In order for them to become independent writers, they will need to know how to use different resources that are available to them. Knowing how to get information and being able to use it will give children more confidence in their writing abilities.

Teaching the Lesson

- Explain to children that you will be writing about how to wash your hands (or any other topic). Then begin writing on an easel pad. As you are writing, read the words aloud. *I want to wash my . . . I want to write the word* hands, *but I don't know how to spell it. What can I do?* Elicit some responses. You may get answers such as *sound it out, look on the Word Wall,* or *ask the teacher. Yes, you can do all of those things. The Word Wall is a very good place to look when you don't know a word. If I want to spell hands, I can look on the Word Wall for the word* and, *add an* h *at the beginning and an* s *at the end, and that makes* hands.
- Reread the sentence and add the word *hands. I want to wash my hands.* Continue on with the next sentence. *I will need some water and . . . I want to write* soap, *but I don't know how to spell that word. The Word Wall won't help me, so where else can I look?*
- Introduce the picture dictionary. *This is called a* dictionary. *In this book there are pictures of things that you might want to spell. I can look in this dictionary, and maybe I will find the word* soap. *I found a picture of soap, so I will copy the word that is next to the picture. I will need some water and soap.* Continue writing two or three more sentences until you finish with the topic.

Teacher Tip

Tailor the Mini-lesson to different Stages of English Language Acquisition and to the needs of the children in your classroom.

Extending the lesson

When children are ready, invite them to use other resources, such as their own dictionaries, other Word Walls or pictorial lists, and words found around the room that will help them with their writing. Encourage children to use a dictionary or thesaurus to find replacement words or synonyms. Show children how to use the guide words when consulting a dictionary for spelling.

Assessment Connection

As you are looking at children's writing, see if there are words that are misspelled that children could find using the different resources.

On Your Own

Options for **STAGES**

❸ Have children in this Stage write a few phrases or sentences. Encourage them to use their resources to help them with their writing.

❹❺ Have children in these Stages look at some of the writing they have already done for words they did not know how to spell. Have them try to use the resources to fix the words.

TEKS **1.20D** use resources to find correct spellings, synonyms, and replacement words
1.20E use conventional spelling of familiar words

Mini-lesson 49
Editing for Subject-Verb Agreement

Lesson Background
As English language learners are beginning to write, they often have a difficult time with subject-verb agreement. This Mini-lesson will deal with regular present tense subjects and verbs. Prior to beginning this Mini-lesson, be sure to complete both the "Naming Words" and "Action Words" Mini-lessons on pages 51 and 54.

Teaching the Lesson
- Explain to children that when you write, the naming word has to go with the action word. Demonstrate this with the following activity, using the verb (action word) *jump*.
- As you are jumping, say *I jump*. Write *I jump* on the board. Next have a boy jump. As he is jumping, say *He jumps*. Write *He jumps* on the board. Continue by having a girl jump (*She jumps*) and two children jump (*They jump*).
- Point out to children that when they are writing, they should try to put the correct ending on each action word.

Extending the Lesson
Do the same activity with other regular present-tense action words (*run, walk, write,* and so on).

On Your Own

Options for **STAGES**

❸ Explain to children in this Stage that you have written four sentences with a word missing in each sentence. Tell children that they are going to decide whether the word *eat* or *eats* should be written in the blank.

I ____ an apple.
He ____ an apple.
She ____ an apple.
They ____ an apple.

❹ ❺ Have children in these Stages look at their previous writing to see if they need to fix any of their action words. Have children use resources to make sure the action words are spelled correctly.

Assessment Connection
As you observe children's writing, look to see if they are using the proper subject-verb agreement. Keep in mind that not every single mistake needs to be scrutinized.

TEKS **1.19D** revise selected drafts for varied purposes
1.20B write with more proficient spelling of inflectional endings
1.20E use conventional spelling of familiar words
1.21B compose complete sentences and use appropriate end punctuation

Mini-lesson 50
Fixing Word Order

Teacher Tip

Use this Mini-lesson to build on your shared writing lessons whenever the opportunity arises in the classroom.

Assessment Connection

Children for whom English is a second language frequently experience difficulty with correct sentence order, such as placement of adjectives, prepositional phrases, and pronouns. Be aware of this problem as you assess children's writing.

Lesson Background

As English language learners are beginning to write, they will sometimes put words in the wrong order. This is due in part to their home languages. For example, a Spanish-speaking child might write *I like to eat an apple red*, because in Spanish the adjective comes after the noun. This Mini-lesson will show children that when they edit a written piece in English, they should look for errors in word order. It is important for you to remember that while children are writing their first drafts, they should be focusing on getting their meaning across rather than correct word order.

Teaching the Lesson

- To prepare for the lesson, write the sentences below on sentence strips. Then cut each apart to make individual word cards. Store each set of words in a separate envelope.

My friend has a white cat.

The dog ate a big bone.

- Place the words of the first sentence in the pocket chart, mixing them up: *My friend has a cat white.* Read the sentence aloud. *Can anyone tell me what is wrong in this sentence?* Elicit responses. *That's right, in English we put the describing word before the naming word.* Read the sentence aloud. *So now it says* My friend has a *white* cat. *That is why it is important when you go back to edit your writing that you read the writing aloud to yourself or a friend.*
- *As you are reading it aloud, you might ask yourself, "Is that the way (Nina) would say it?" Don't worry about this when you are writing a first draft. You can fix any mistakes you make when you go back and edit.*

Extending the Lesson

Do the same activity with the second sentence, mixing up the words so that they read: *My dog ate a bone big.*

On Your Own

Options for STAGES

❸ Choose a piece of writing for each child in this Stage to correct. If children don't have any work to correct, divide a simple sentence on word cards and have them put the cards in the correct order.

❹❺ Have children in these Stages look back at earlier work to see if they need to edit for correct word order.

Mini-lesson 51
Matching Words and Pictures

Lesson Background

One aspect of the editing process for English language learners is checking to make sure their words and pictures match. This Mini-lesson uses "silly sentences" to help children become more aware of how important it is to check their writing against their illustrations.

Teaching the Lesson

- To prepare for this Mini-lesson, find several large, detailed magazine illustrations. Cut out each illustration and glue it to a piece of construction paper. Then write a "silly sentence" under the picture. The sentence should come close to matching the picture, but should be off in some way. For example, for a magazine picture that shows a cat eating cat food, you might write *The black cat is eating the sock.*

- *I found some pictures I like in these old magazines. I put them on construction paper and then wrote sentences to go with the pictures. Now I'd like to share them with you.* Display the first picture and invite children to join in as you read the sentence aloud. *Hmmm . . . now that I'm looking at the picture again, I see that my sentence sounds silly. The cat isn't eating the sock. The cat is eating cat food! My picture and words don't match. I'll change them so they do.* Use the delete mark to cross out the word *sock.* Use a caret to insert *cat food. Let's read the sentence together again. Do the picture and words match now? Yes, they do.*

Extending the Lesson

Continue in the same way with one or two other examples.

On Your Own

Options for **STAGES**

❷❸ Put children in these Stages in pairs. Provide pairs with pictures cut out of magazines with simple silly sentences written on them. Have children read the sentences, figure out what is silly about them, and fix them using the delete marks and caret symbols.

❹❺ Have children in these Stages choose pictures from a magazine, write silly sentences, and trade with a partner. Then have them fix each other's sentences. Have children use resources to check the spelling of words.

Have children share their sentences with you when they have finished correcting them. Remind them that they should always check their words against their pictures.

You Will Need

- ✔ old magazines
- ✔ magazine pictures with simple silly sentences written on them (for Stages 2 and 3)
- ✔ scissors
- ✔ 12" x 18" construction paper
- ✔ glue
- ✔ writing paper

Assessment Connection

When conferencing with children, have them share illustrations as well as words. When possible, ask them to explain how the pictures go with the words and the words go with the pictures.

TEKS
1.18C write to record ideas and reflections
1.19D revise selected drafts for varied purposes
1.20E use conventional spelling of familiar words
1.22B respond constructively to others' writing
1.23B record or dictate own knowledge of a topic in various ways

Mini-lesson 52
Writing for an Audience

You Will Need

✔ three pieces of your writing:
- a letter to someone
- a journal entry
- a book response

Teacher Tip

Tailor the Mini-lesson to different Stages of English Language Acquisition and to the needs of the children in your classroom.

Assessment Connection

Look at work children have determined is ready for an audience. Note whether they have chosen an appropriate audience.

Lesson Background

As English language learners become comfortable in their roles as authors, they often want to share everything they have written. This Mini-lesson will help them to consider the audience before writing and create a piece for that audience.

Teaching the Lesson

- Read your writing samples to children. Explain that you have finished these pieces and are ready to share them with the audience you had in mind when you wrote each piece.
- Invite children to identify the audience you had in mind when you wrote each piece. *Would my friends be interested in reading this? What about the principal? How about my parents? Did I write this for someone special?* As children identify the audience for each piece, explain your thought process as you wrote it, for example, *I knew that my friends would enjoy hearing about the baseball game, so I made sure to include it in my letter to them.*
- Explain to children that when we write, we have to think about who will read our finished pieces and write so that those people will enjoy our work.
- Put each piece aside to be used with the Mini-lesson *A Classroom Publishing Plan* on page 75. Explain your classroom system for storing writing that will not be published.

Extending the Lesson

Bring in several nonfiction books on a wide range of topics. As you share each title with children, ask them who might find the book interesting.

On Your Own

Have children write a letter to the principal. As children write, remind them to keep the principal in mind and write so that he or she will enjoy the letter.

Options for **STAGES**

❸ Children in this Stage can write a few phrases or short sentences to the principal.	❹❺ Children in these Stages can write complete sentences with the principal in mind.

TEKS 1.18E write to communicate with a variety of audiences
1.19D revise selected drafts for varied purposes
1.22C determine how own writing achieves its purposes

A Classroom Publishing Plan

Lesson Background

As English language learners begin to enter the publishing part of the writing process, it is important to have a publishing system available to them. A piece of writing that is published can go a long way toward motivating young writers. By publishing children's writing, we are validating their efforts and celebrating their successes.

Teaching the Lesson

- *Today we are going to learn about becoming published authors. Many of you have a lot of things you have written. You have put some of those papers in your writing folders. You have taken some of them home to share with your family. You have even shared some of your writing with friends in the classroom or with me. Now we are going to learn how to take the things we have written and make them into books like these authors did.*

- Hold up the trade books you have gathered. *Sometimes we write things that we want a lot of people to read and enjoy. We want to take what we've written and make them into books with pictures, so others can read them. I am going to show you how what I wrote can be made into a book that I can share with you and put on our reading shelf for everyone to read.*

  At this point share your classroom publishing system with children. Think about the following questions as you set up your system.

- Who will help put the child's writing into book format? Will technology be available for children to compose text? Will children be able to use spell check? Will children be able to print out their work?

- How will the child make the decision to publish? Once this decision is made, how will you be notified? A basket labeled *To Be Published*? A publishing folder for each child? Through a one-on-one conference?

- What format will the published piece take? Handwritten on pages that are stapled together? Composed text with available technology? Bound together with a binding machine?

Extending the Lesson

As a class, brainstorm ways to choose what written pieces children want to publish. To help children choose, use the Writing Rubric for English Language Writers, pages 18–19, as a guide.

On Your Own

Options for **STAGES**

| ❸ Have children in this Stage look back at something they have written and publish it. | ❹ ❺ Have children in these Stages write something new to be published. |

You Will Need

- ✔ examples of favorite classroom trade titles
- ✔ something you have written
- ✔ children's own work (Stage 3)
- ✔ paper; one per child (Stages 4 and 5)

Assessment Connection

Note whether children are able to follow the steps of the classroom publishing system.

TEKS
1.19E use technology to compose text
1.20E use conventional spelling of familiar words
1.22A identify the most effective features of a piece of writing
1.22C determine how own writing achieves its purposes

Mini-lesson 54
Choosing a Title

You Will Need

✔ a short untitled piece of writing

✔ easel pad

✔ markers

Teacher Tip

Revisit this Mini-lesson often until children show evidence of incorporating the instruction in their writing.

Assessment Connection

Have children share their writing and titles with you. Assess whether or not titles match the content. Ask children to explain why they chose their titles.

Lesson Background

English language learners often write labels as their titles rather than creating a title that captures the reader's attention, or they do not give their writing a title at all. This lesson will model the thinking process involved in choosing an appropriate title for one's writing.

Teaching the Lesson

- Read what you have written aloud to children. After you finish, explain that you need to give the piece a title. Explain what a title is if children do not already know. Explain that authors often wait until they are finished to give their writing a title. They do that because they want to make sure the title goes with the writing.

- Tell children that you are going to list some ideas, and you would like their help in choosing the best title for your writing. Begin listing possible titles, saying each aloud as you write it. Include one title that has little or nothing to do with the topic of the piece of writing.

- After completing the list, reread each title. Ask questions about each one. *Do you think this is a good title for my writing? Why (or Why not)?* Help them conclude that one title would be a bad choice because it does not go with the writing. Cross out that title, using the delete mark. Then explain that the author gets to make the final decision about the title. Decide upon a title and explain why you chose it. Add the title to the writing, explaining that you put a title at the top of the paper or on the cover of a book.

Extending the Lesson

Do the same activity with a different piece of writing.

On Your Own

Options for STAGES

❸ For each child in this Stage, choose a piece of writing that needs a title. Then put them in pairs and have them help each other create titles for their pieces.

❹❺ Have children in these Stages choose an untitled piece of writing from their journals or writing portfolios. Ask each child to think of a title for that piece.

TEKS
1.18D write to discover, develop, and refine ideas
1.19D revise selected drafts for varied purposes
1.22C determine how own writing achieves its purposes
1.24C monitor language production and employ self-corrective techniques

Mini-lesson 55
Making a Cover/Binding

Lesson Background
Part of the fun of publishing is making a cover for a book. English language learners can make a cover for an individual writing piece or put together several pieces of writing and make them into a book.

Teaching the Lesson
- Children love to make their writing look authentic by adding front and back covers. Before they do so, however, they should understand what makes a good book cover. Display the familiar books.
- Review the elements of the cover—an illustration that tells something about the story, a title, and the names of the author and illustrator. Discuss with children whether or not the cover illustrations go with the stories as they remember them.

Extending the Lesson
Show children a cover that you have made for a piece of writing. Help children use a computer to create the cover.

On Your Own

Options for **STAGES**

| ❸ Choose a piece of finished writing for each child in this Stage. | ❹❺ Ask each child in these Stages to choose a piece of writing they have finished or on which they are working. |

- Invite children to make covers for their writing. Distribute cover paper. Help children write their titles on the front covers. (If they have not yet chosen titles, see the Mini-lesson "Choosing a Title" on page 76.)
- Have them add their own names as author/illustrators. Then ask children to think about their writing. Have them pick a person, scene, or event from the writing. Then have them choose a cover idea from the pictures that come to mind. They can use crayons or markers to draw their illustrations. If children are making covers for finished work, help them put the covers and book pages together.

You Will Need
- ✔ selection of familiar books with interesting covers
- ✔ paper for making covers
- ✔ markers and/or crayons
- ✔ a cover that you have made for a piece of writing

Assessment Connection
As you are looking at the covers, make sure that children have an appropriate title and drawing to go with their writing. If not, discuss what they can do to make it better.

TEKS **1.19E** use technology to compose text
1.22A identify the most effective features of a piece of writing
1.22C determine how own writing achieves its purposes
1.23B record or dictate own knowledge of a topic in various ways

Mini-lesson 56
Author's Chair

Teacher Tip

Tailor the Mini-lesson to different Stages of English Language Acquisition and to the needs of the children in your classroom.

Assessment Connection

Observe children as they use the Author's chair. Encourage those who seem reluctant to share their work to give the chair a try.

Lesson Background

English language learners will show even more pride in their work when it is obviously valued by others. This Mini-lesson introduces them to the concept of the Author's chair—a special spot where they can be recognized as authors and can share their writing with others.

Teaching the Lesson

- Display a variety of familiar trade books. Select books whose authors are familiar to children—you may want to limit the number of authors and have two or three books by each. *We have talked a lot about writing and being authors. These books are by some of your favorite authors. Do you remember who the authors are? Besides writing words, there is another important job when making books like these. The other important person is the illustrator. Who can tell me what the illustrator does?* Elicit responses from children. Point out an example in the selected books. *Sometimes the author is the illustrator too.* Point out an example of an author/illustrator.

- *You are the author and the illustrator of your own writing. So you have two reasons to be proud of your work. I am proud of your work too, and I would like you to have a special place where you can share it. That's why we are going to have an Author's chair.* Place the sign on the chair you are designating as the Author's chair. *This is where you can sit when you want to share something that you have written.* If you are going to have children sign up to use the chair, explain the procedure at this point.

- Model using the chair yourself and read something that you have written. Invite a volunteer to share a writing sample. Invite others to say what they liked about the writing.

Extending the Lesson

Brainstorm with children a list of rules for the use of the Author's chair.

On Your Own

Distribute a decorative sticker to each child. *Now think about what you would like to share if you choose to sit in the Author's chair. Look through your journal or writing portfolio to find a finished piece of writing you might like to share. Use the sticker to mark that page.* Then invite a few children to share their work from the Author's chair. Present each with an *I am an author* sticker to wear.

Options for **STAGES**

❷ Have children in this Stage show a picture that may or may not have words on it, and then, when possible, have them talk about the picture.

❸❹❺ Have children in these Stages read what they wrote, whether the writing is made up of phrases or sentences.

 TEKS **1.14F** understand literary terms (author, illustrator)
1.22B respond constructively to others' writing

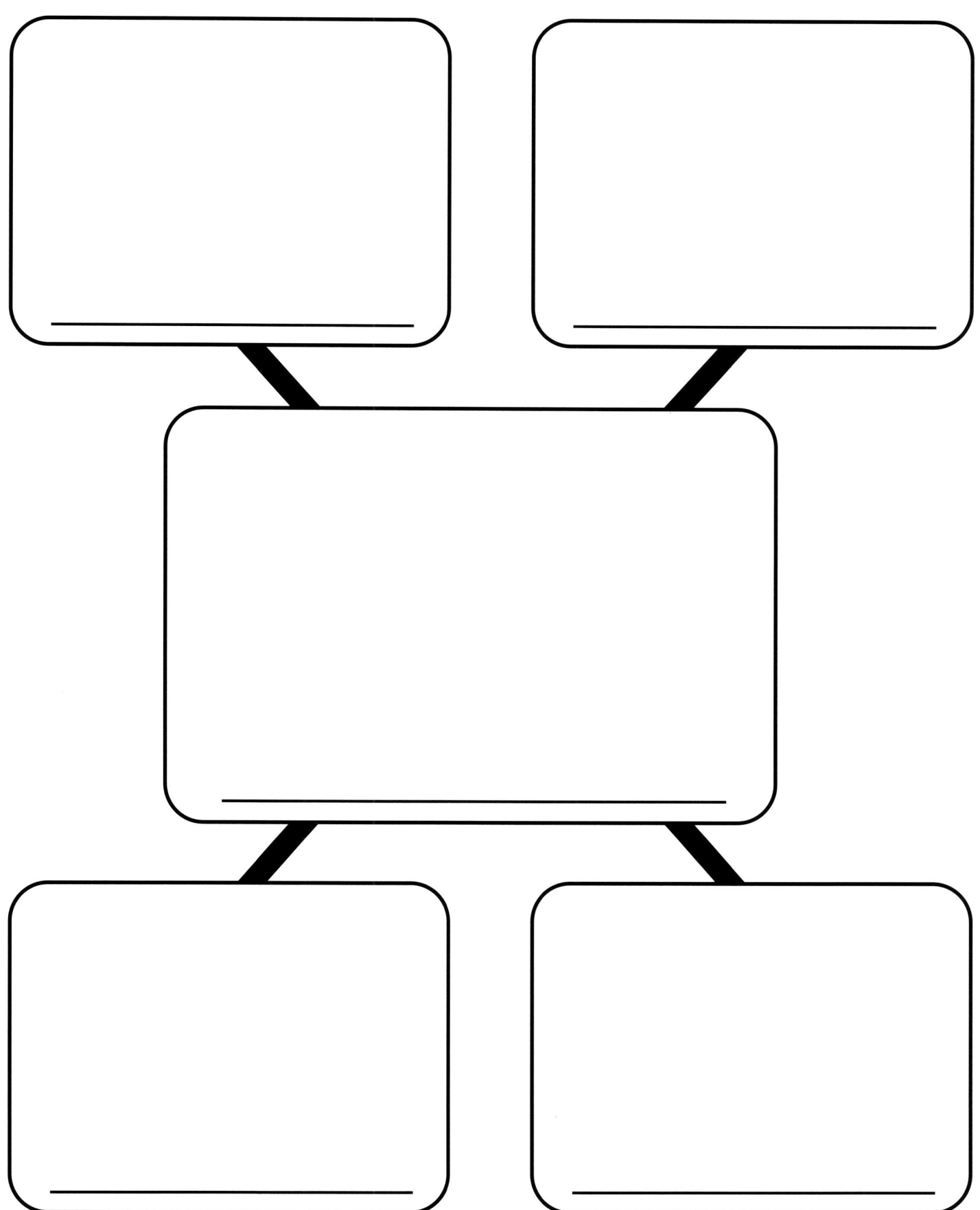

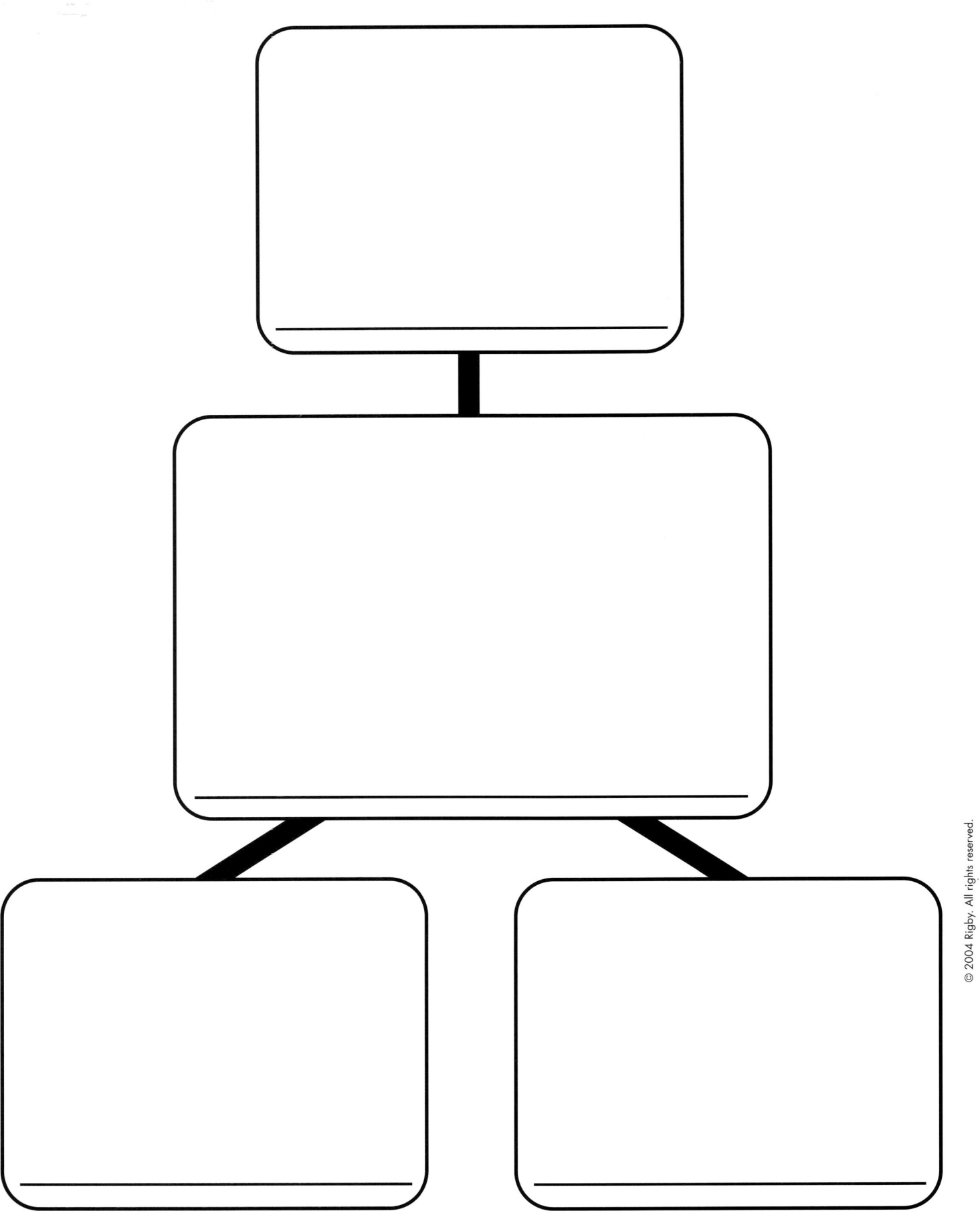

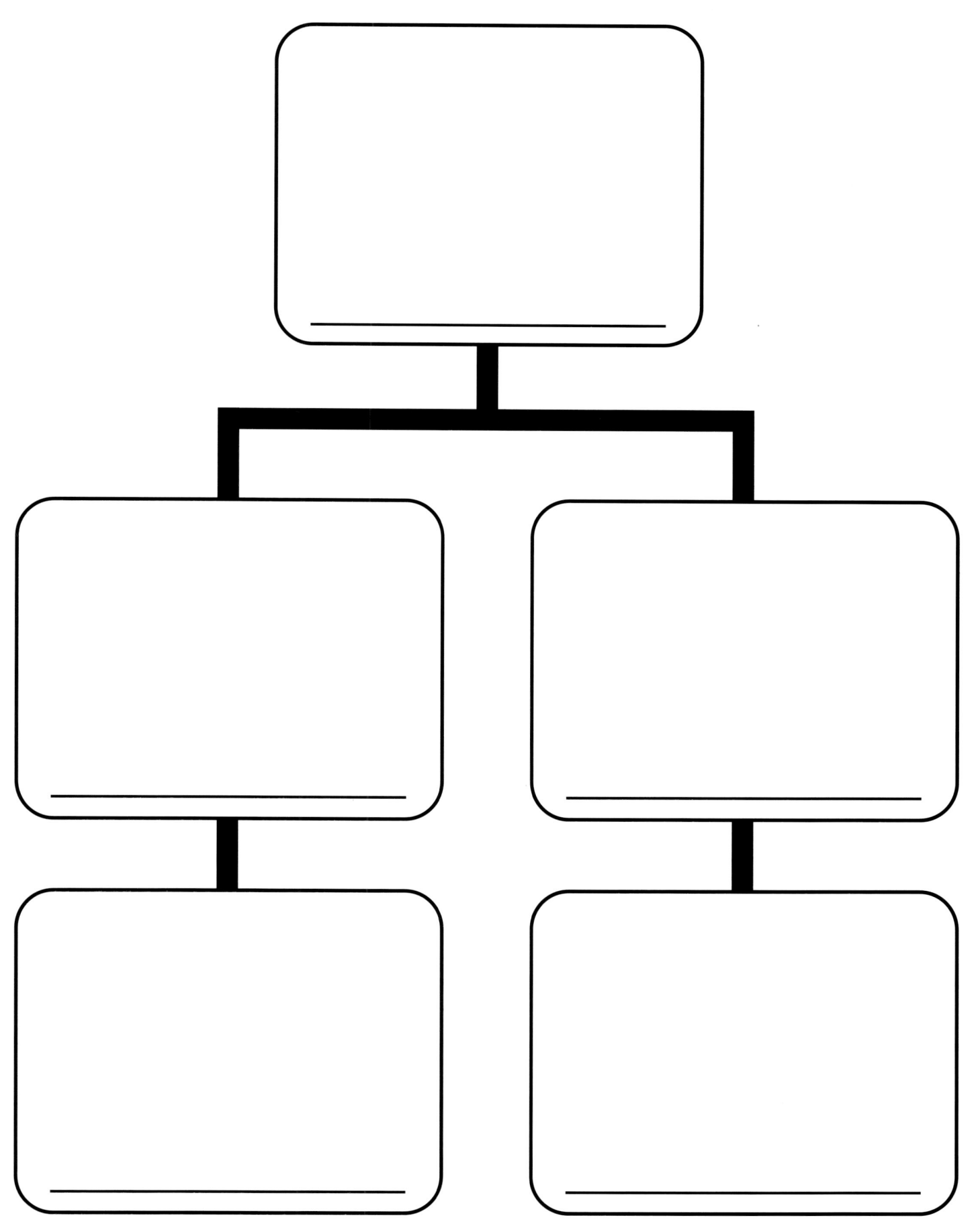

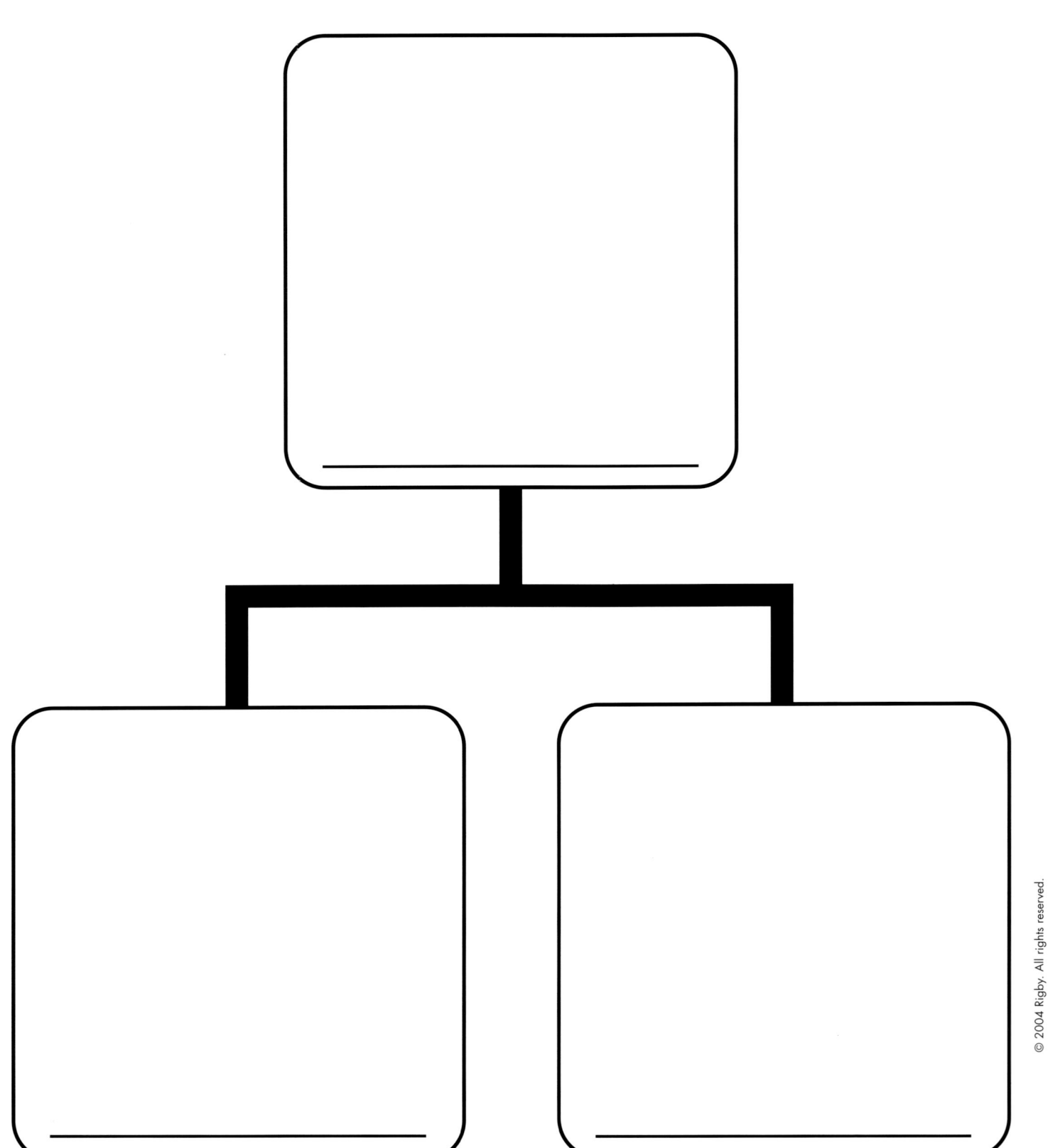

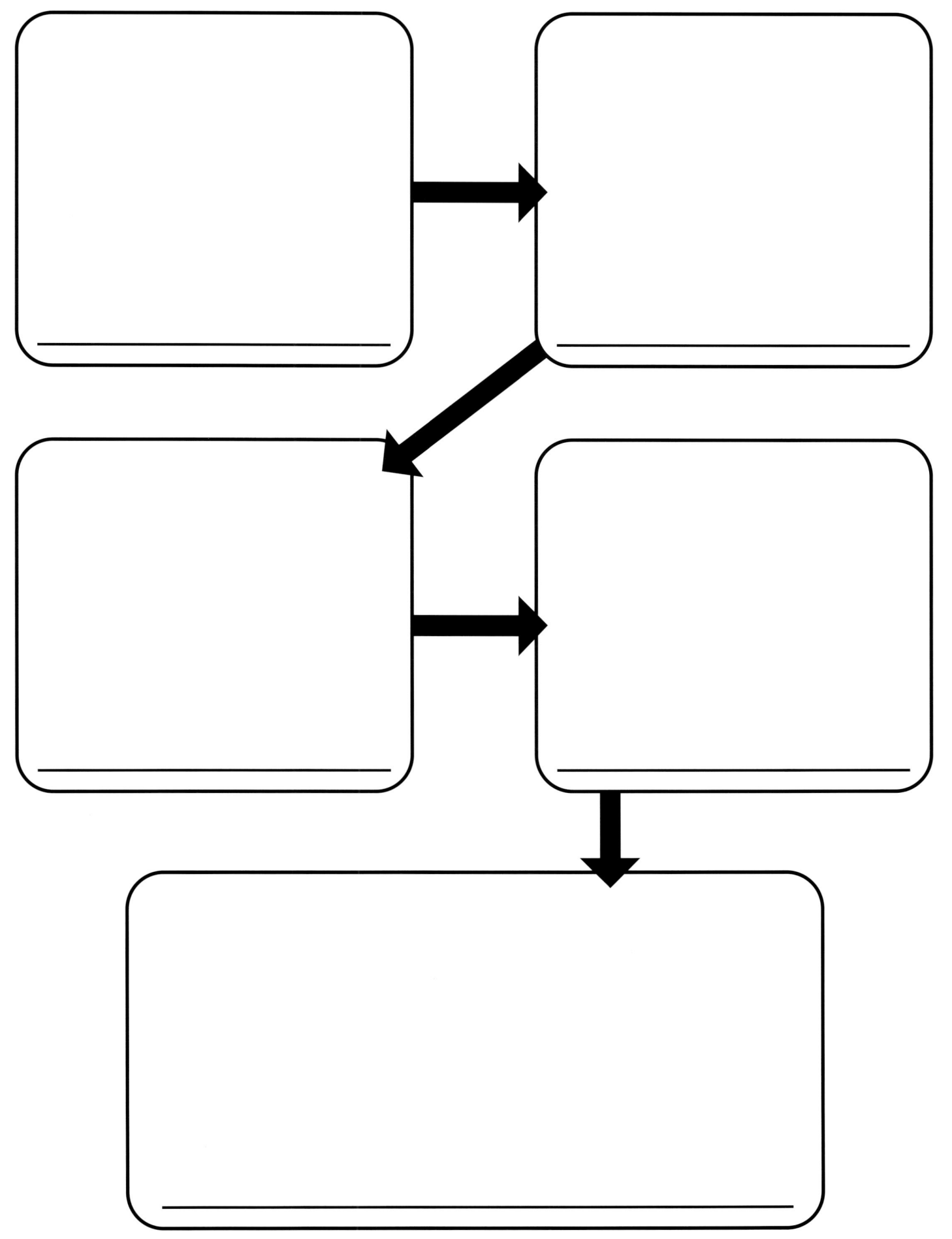

Writing Planner B

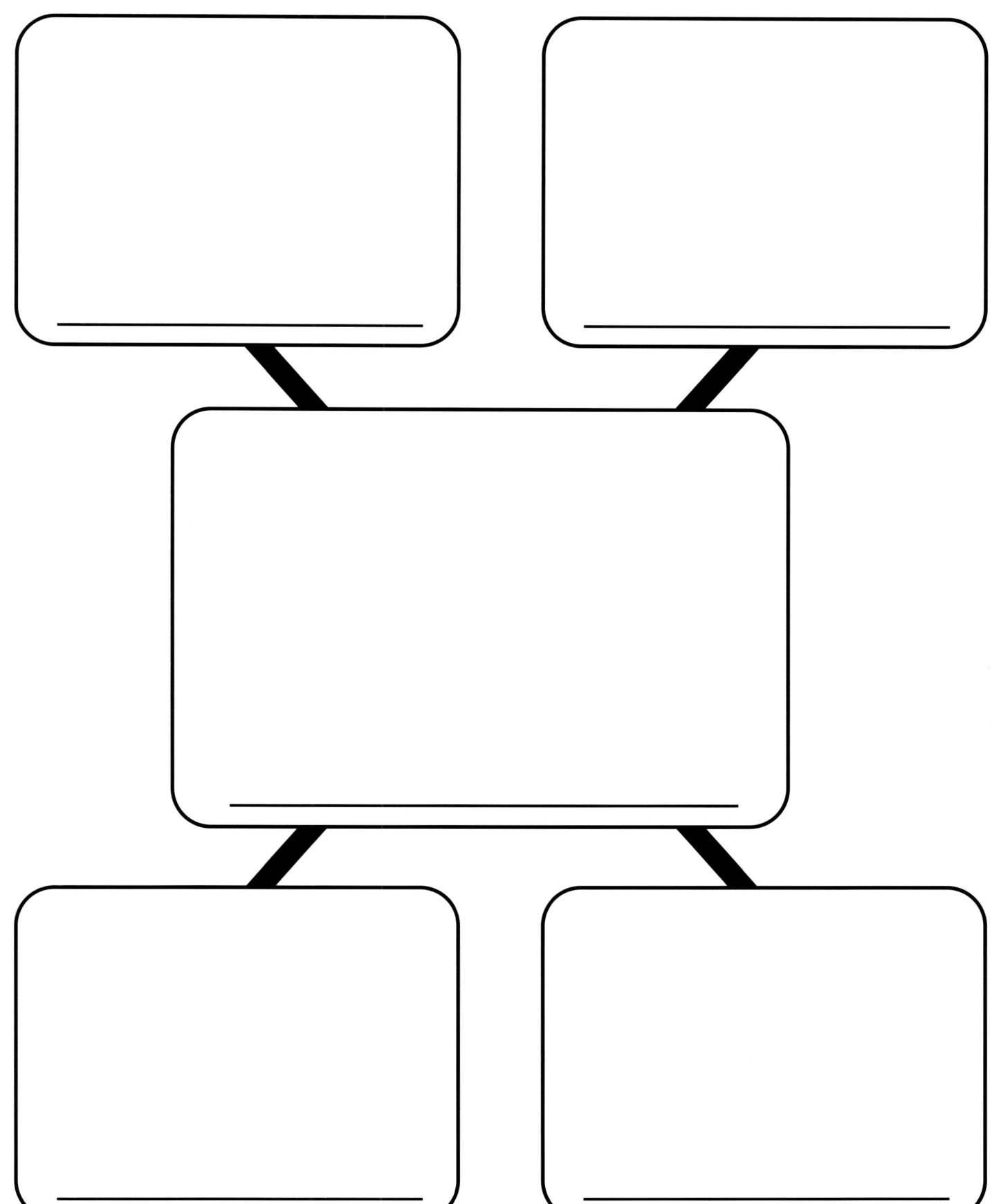

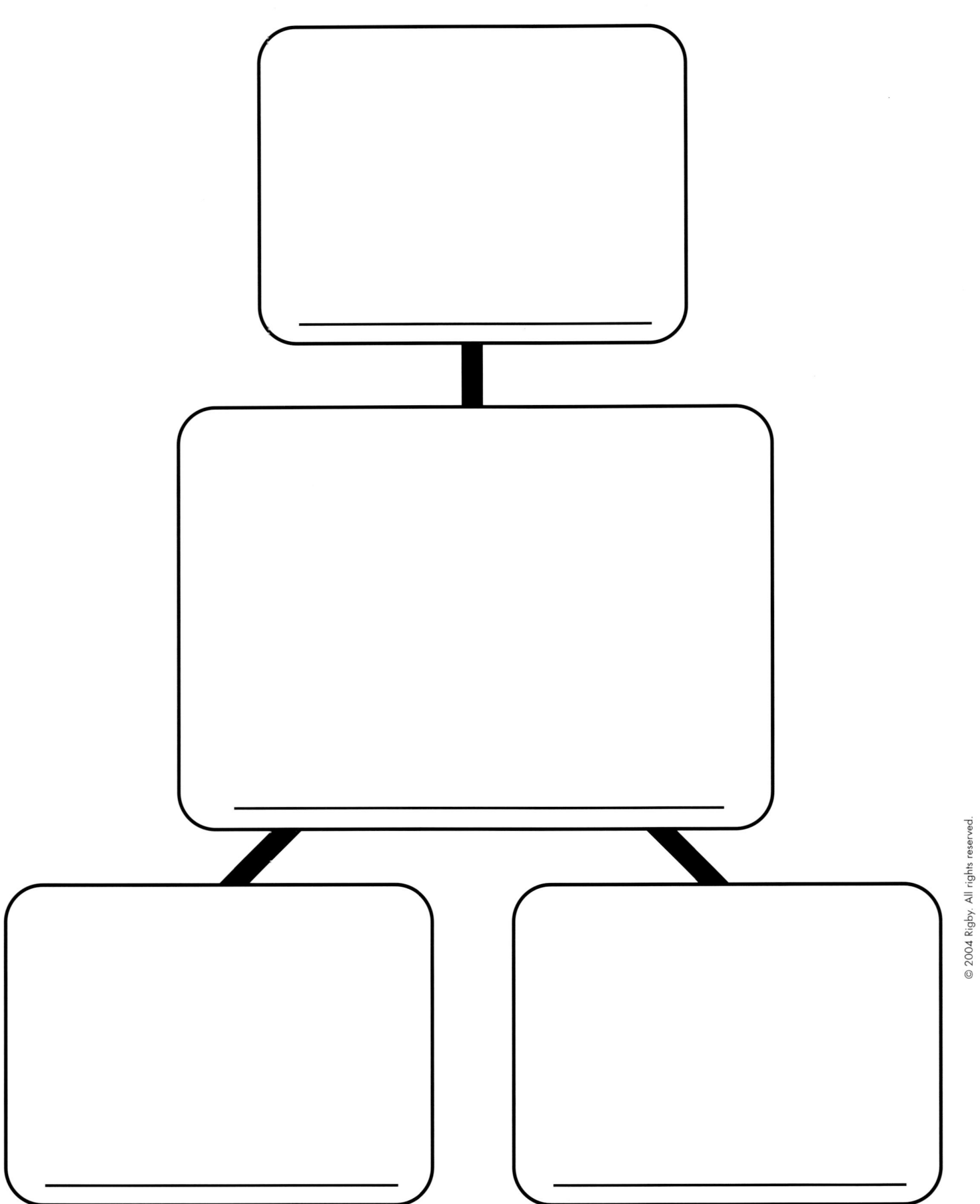

Writing Planner B

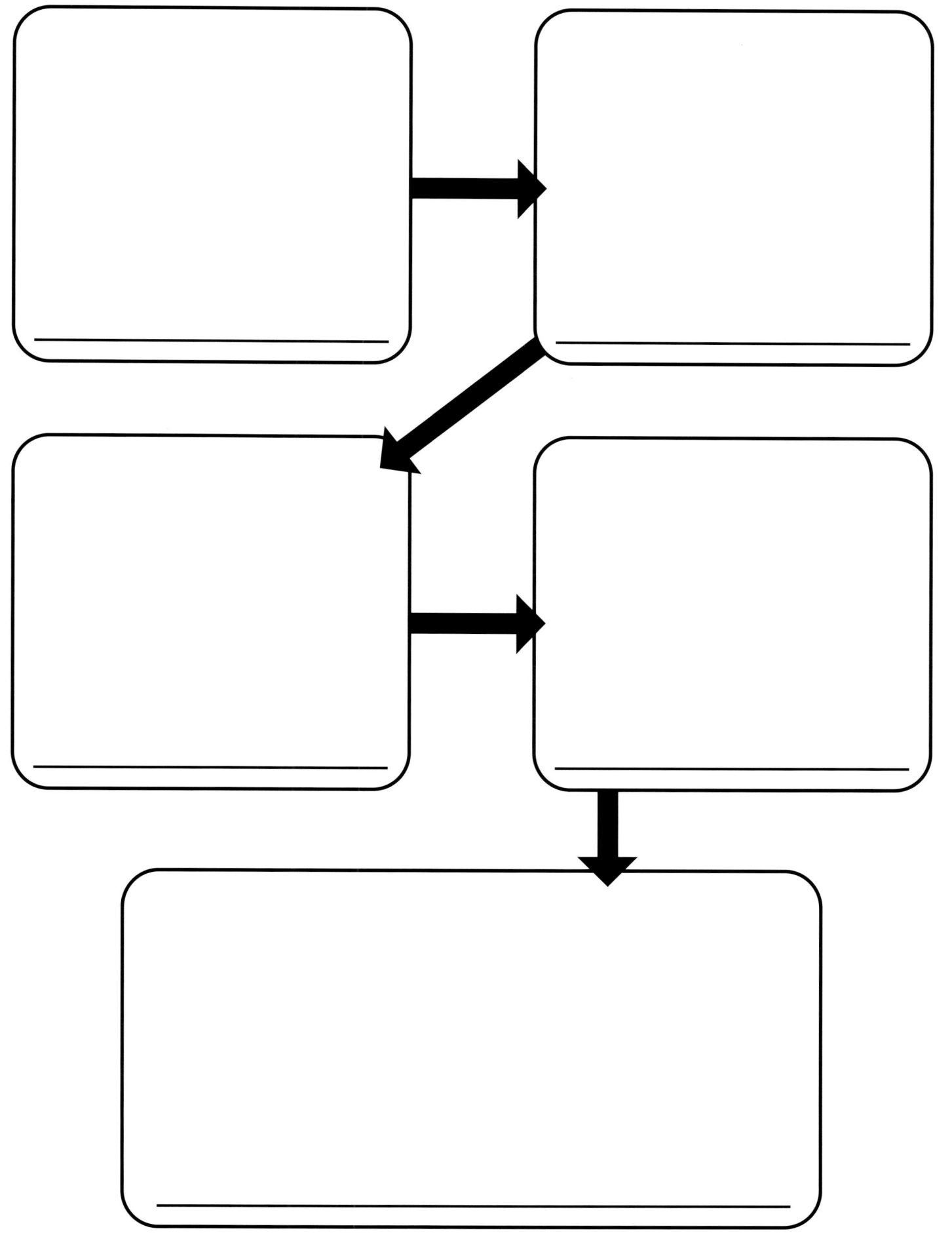

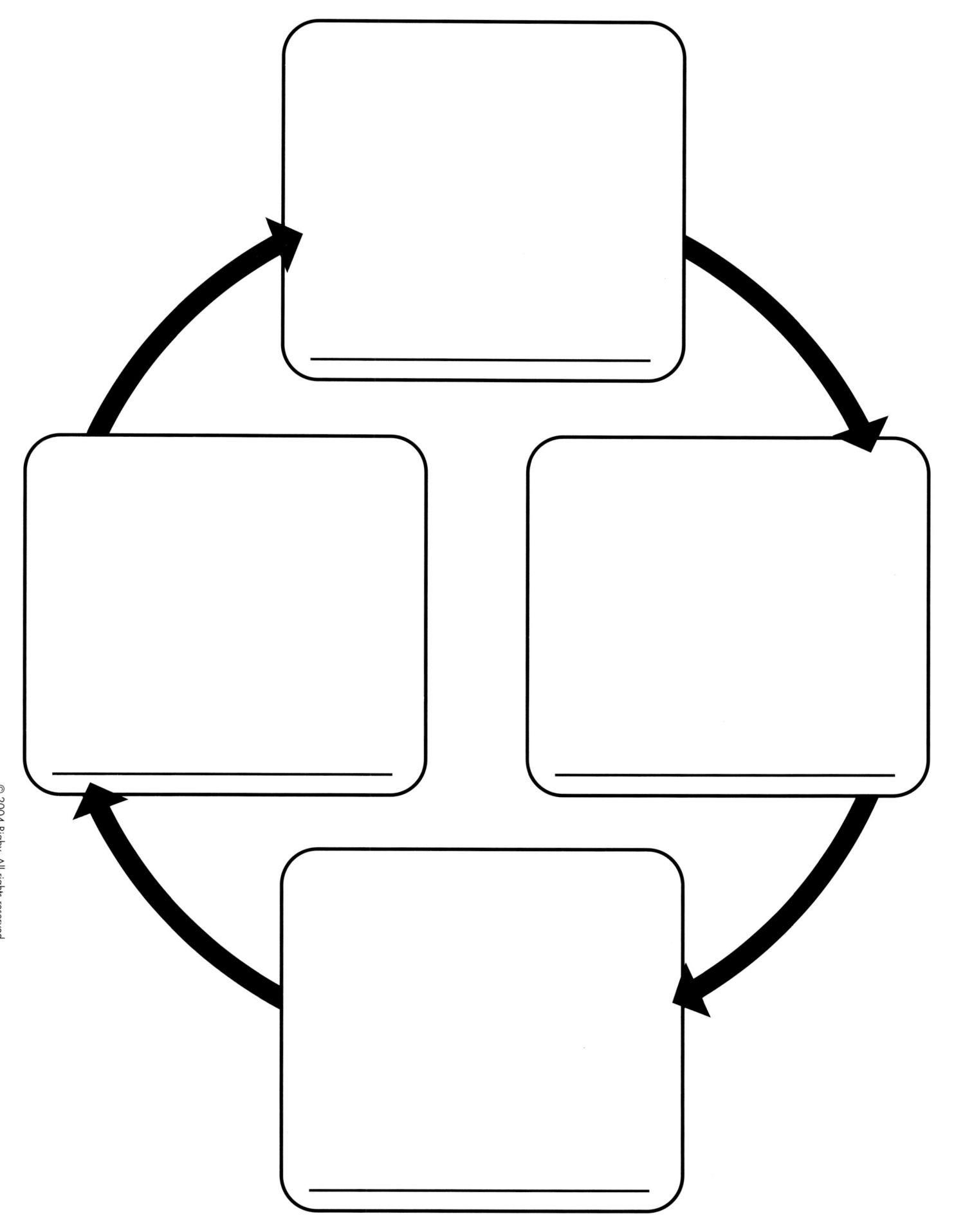

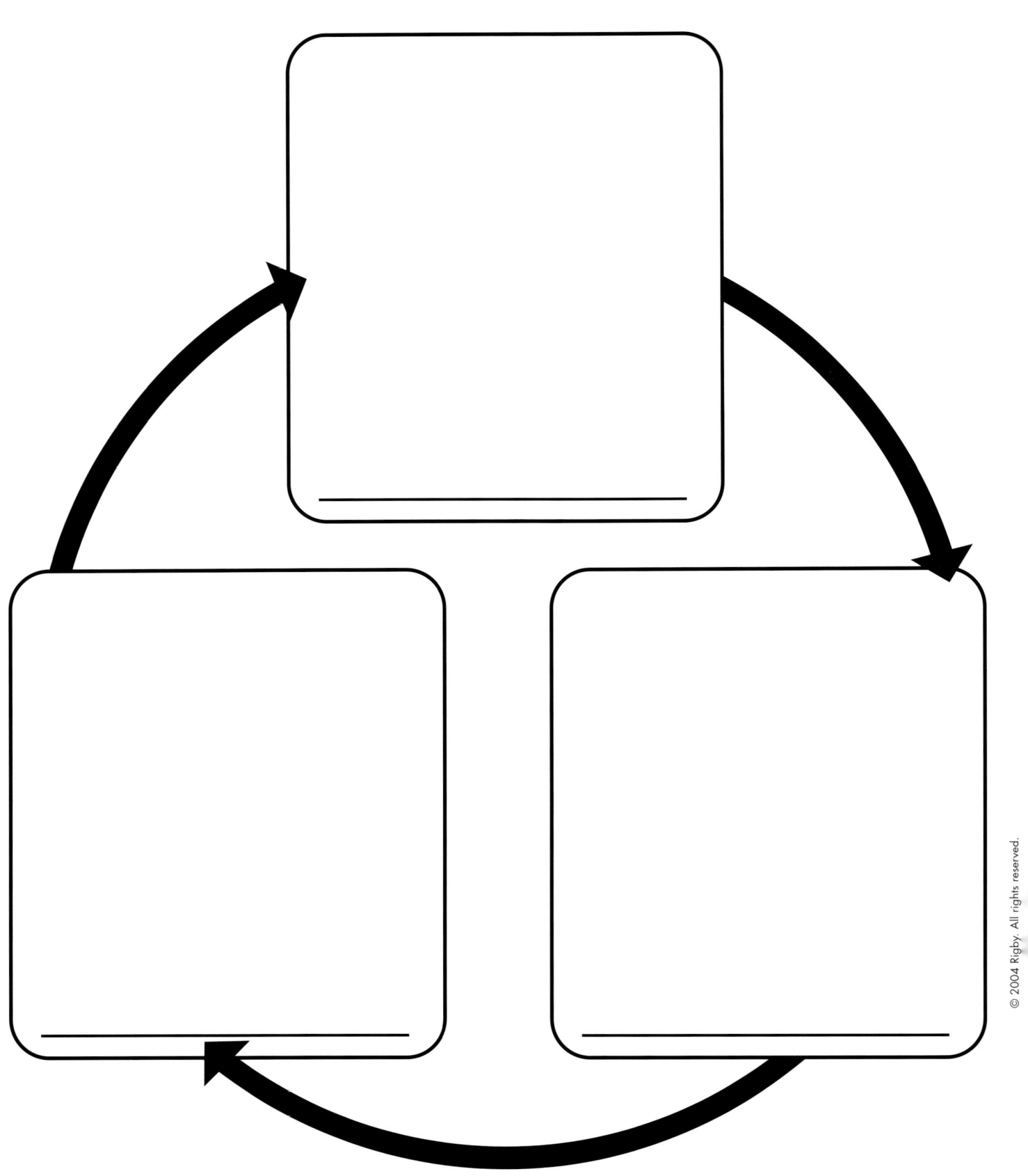

Writing Planner B

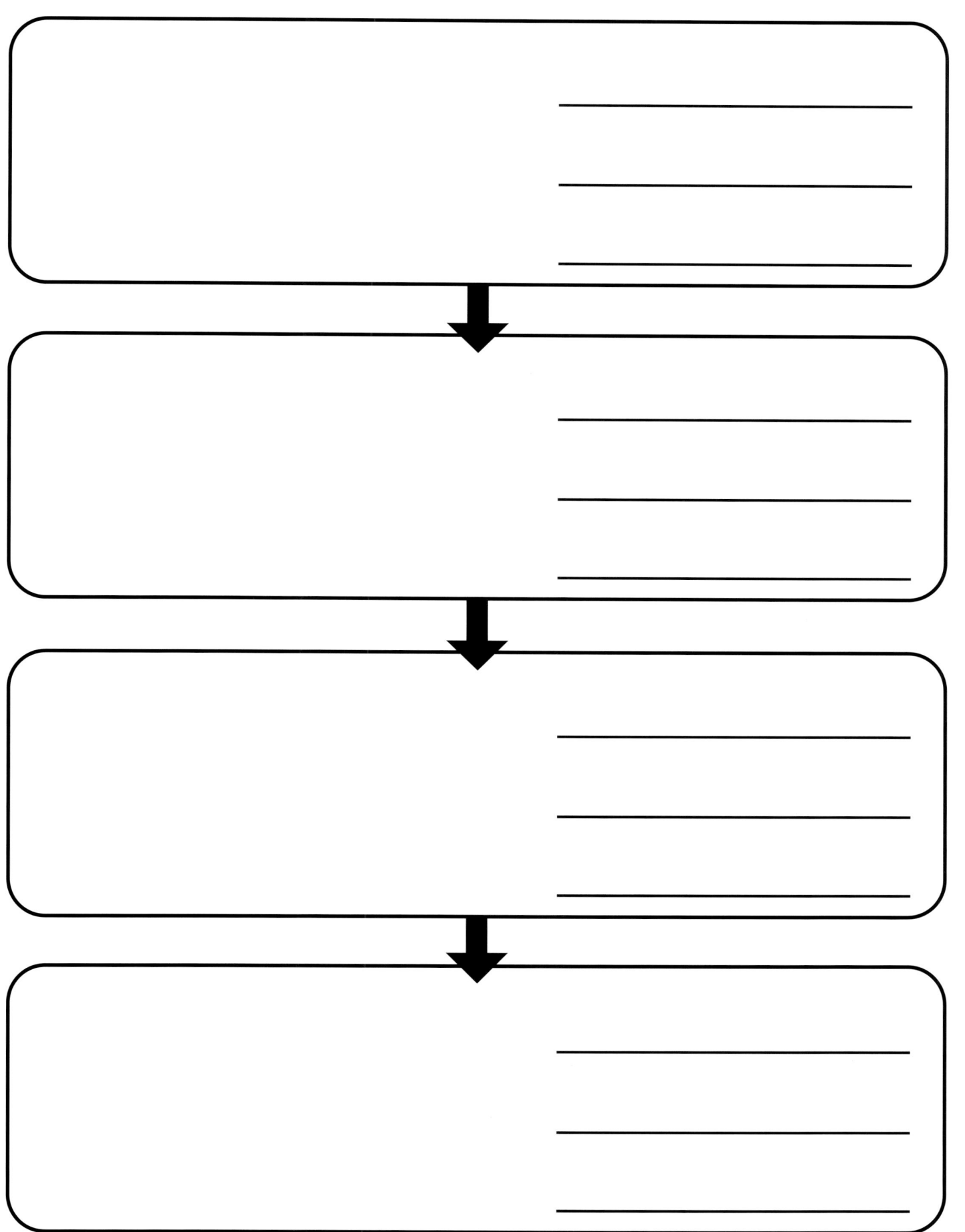

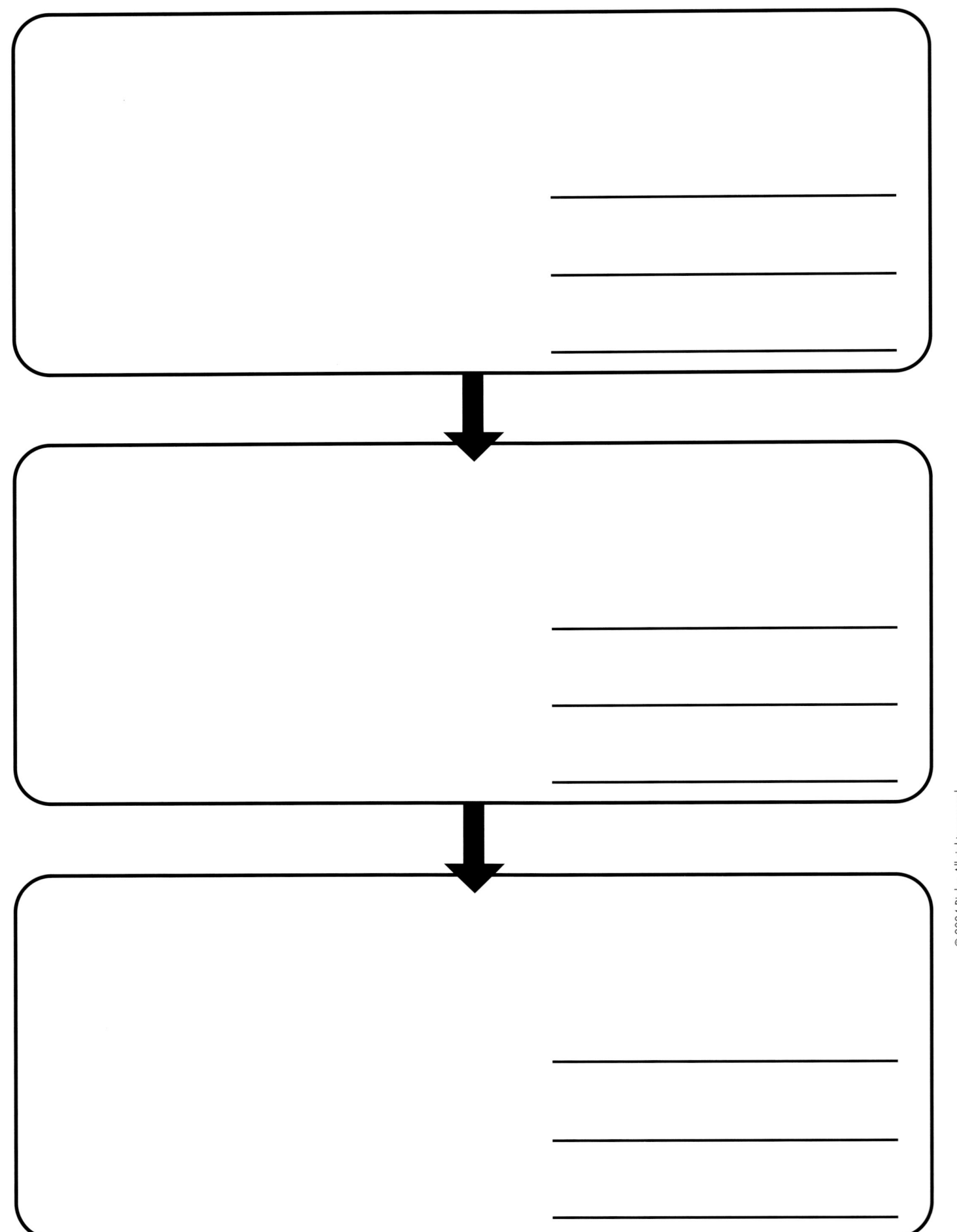

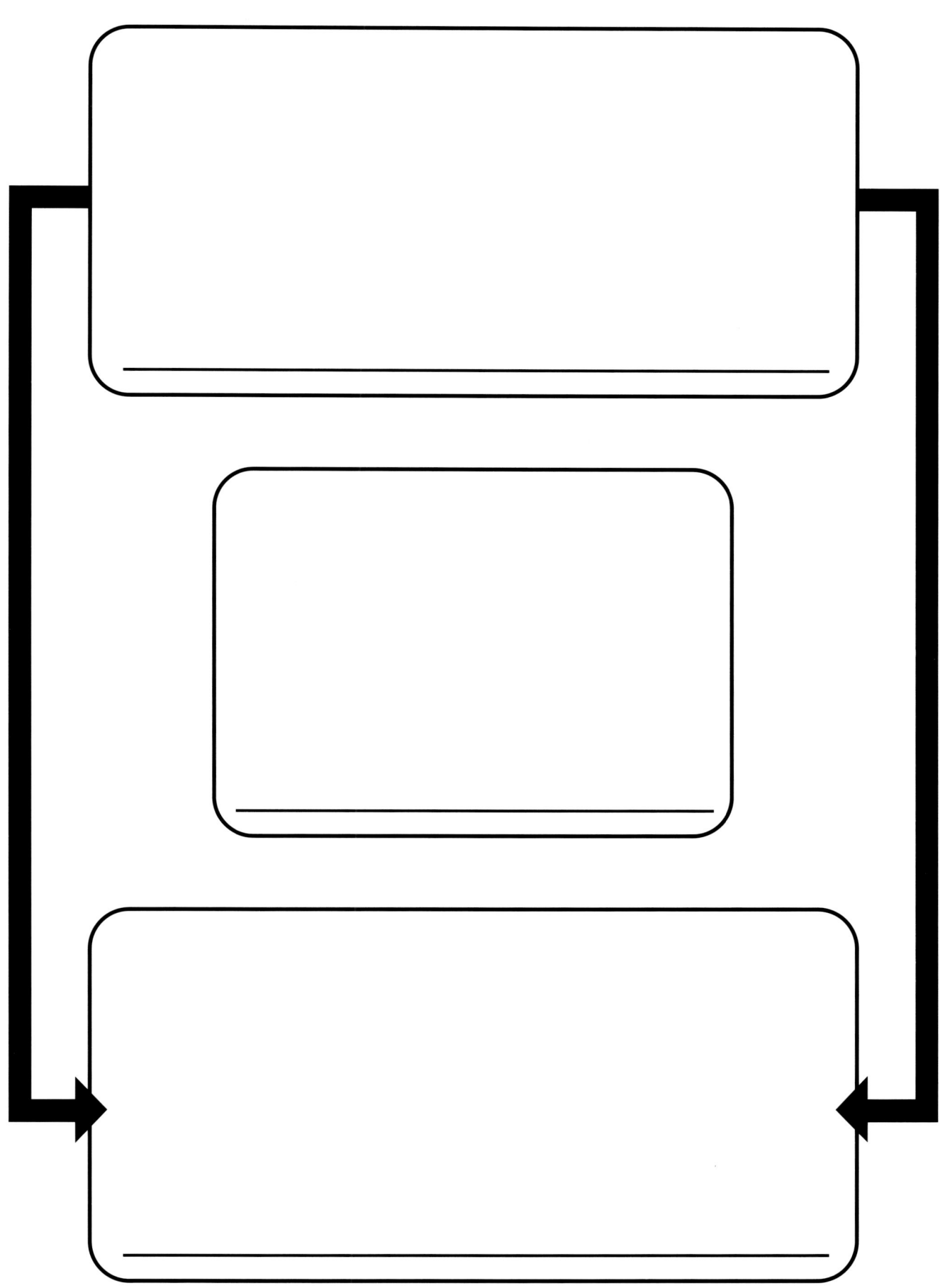

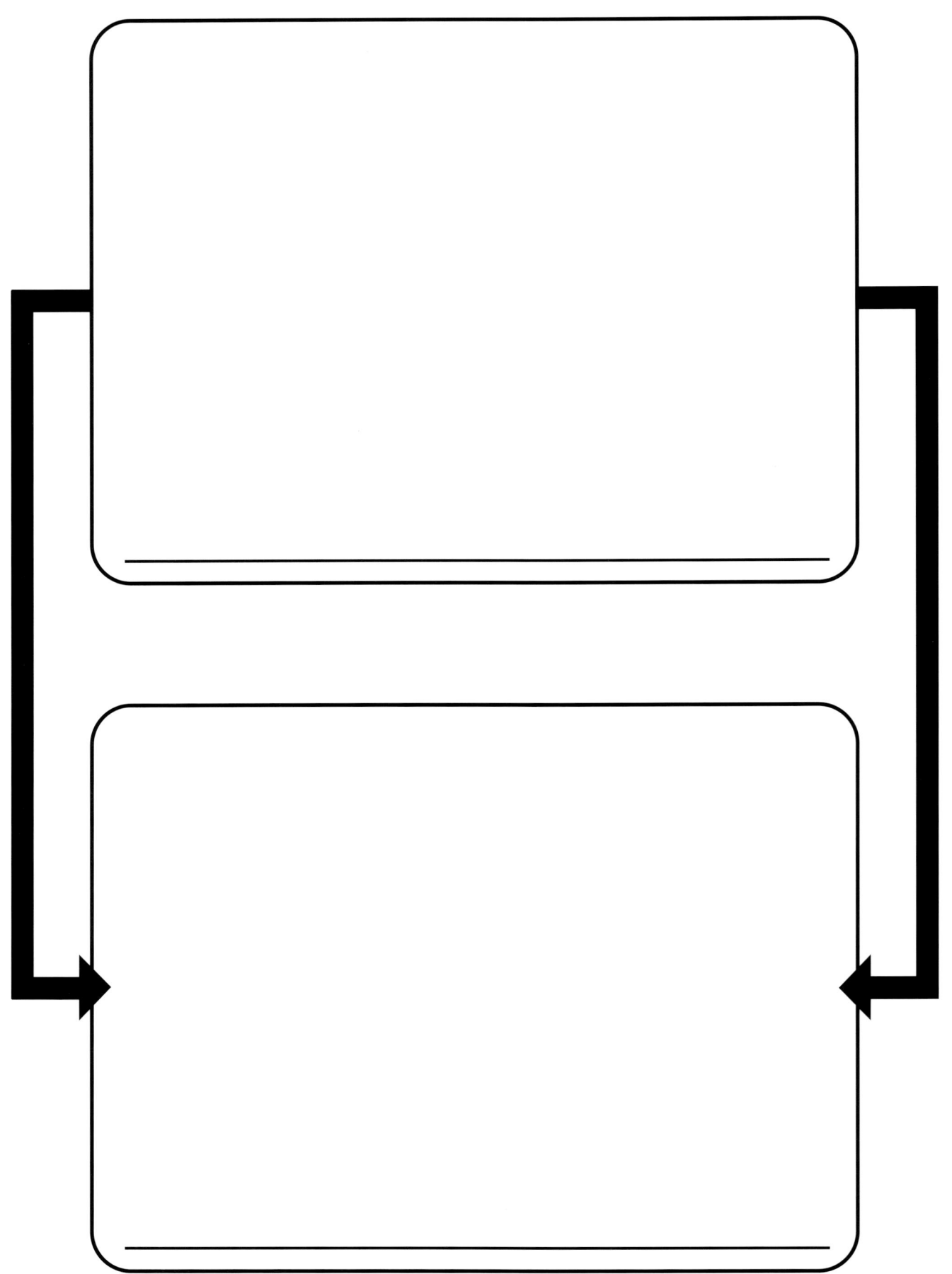

Letter Formation Record

Name:

Grade:

Age:

Date:

Have the child write the lowercase alphabet and the uppercase alphabet on a sheet of paper. Use this form to indicate which letters are written accurately (checkmark) and which ones need further practice (circle).

Key: ___✔___ = formed correctly

___O___ = needs further practice

a	b	c	d	e	f	g
h	i	j	k	l	m	n
o	p	q	r	s	t	u
v	w	x	y	z		
A	B	C	D	E	F	G
H	I	J	K	L	M	N
O	P	Q	R	S	T	U
V	W	X	Y	Z		